PRESENTED TO

_____

BY

_____

_____

_____

DATE

_____

THE
Love Dare
FOR PARENTS

THE
Love Dare
FOR PARENTS

STEPHEN & ALEX
KENDRICK
WITH LAWRENCE KIMBROUGH

B&H
PUBLISHING GROUP

NASHVILLE, TENNESSEE

RECEIVE THIS AS A WARNING.
THIS FORTY-DAY JOURNEY CANNOT
BE TAKEN LIGHTLY.

IT IS A CHALLENGING AND OFTEN
DIFFICULT PROCESS, BUT AN INCREDIBLY
FULFILLING ONE. TO TAKE THIS DARE
REQUIRES A RESOLUTE MIND AND
A STEADFAST DETERMINATION.

IT IS NOT MEANT TO BE SAMPLED OR BRIEFLY
TESTED, AND THOSE WHO QUIT EARLY WILL
FORFEIT THE GREATEST BENEFITS. IF YOU
WILL COMMIT TO A DAY AT A TIME FOR FORTY
DAYS, THE RESULTS COULD CHANGE YOUR
LIFE AND YOUR CHILDREN.

CONSIDER IT A DARE, FROM OTHERS
WHO HAVE DONE IT BEFORE YOU.

Prepare for the Journey
Authors' Preface

Since *The Love Dare* was first published in 2008, we've been thrilled that people around the world have been taking the journey and learning to practice principles of love daily in their marriages. Countless e-mails have poured in, sharing how romance is being rekindled, dying marriages are being saved, and eyes are opening to the nature of true, committed love.

Over that time, the number-one request we have received is for a similar journey to be developed for parents to go through with their children. So with much gratitude, we present to you *The Love Dare for Parents*.

Every chapter has been uniquely written to inspire and strengthen moms and dads in their daily interaction with their children. It's the same, unique format as the original *Love Dare*, and yet a completely new journey!

Although we have ten children of our own, we cannot express enough gratitude to our parents, Larry and Rhonwyn Kendrick, who not only raised us in a loving home but shared counsel and ideas with us as we wrote this book. In many ways, their prayer support, faithfulness, and strong example over the years have influenced almost every chapter.

Some of the parenting principles in this book may seem very simple and second nature to you, while others may provide breakthrough concepts for your family. The key is not what you learn but what you actually implement into your relationship with your children on a consistent basis. Truth transforms when it is correctly applied. Anytime you think, "I already know that," you should follow it up with, "But do I *do* that?" We hope this experience will jump-start you into a new, dynamic way of thinking and living.

Every parent sees areas where they need to improve, but we often don't have a plan of action. This book is designed to help busy parents more fully cherish and enjoy all of their children during each season of their lives. Our goal is to help you develop the habit of communicating genuine love to them on a consistent basis.

At the same time, we hope this helps you turn your children's hearts more fully to you and keeps your relationship with them respectful and loving long-term. This experience should also help you more effectively teach and train them to pass on a stronger legacy for future generations.

We have tried to write in such a way that will be meaningful regardless of whether your children are in preschool or in college, but we realize that some days and dares may need to be adapted to the age of your children and your context.

No matter how your child responds, we encourage you to keep going and enjoy the journey! As you begin, here are five questions we would like to go ahead and answer for you:

1. *What if I'm a single parent or my spouse does not want to participate?*

That is perfectly fine. You can easily adapt each dare to your situation. This will be a great opportunity to strengthen your one-on-one relationship with your children as well as your personal parenting skills.

2. *What if I fall behind and can't keep up?*

Don't feel guilty if you can't follow every dare perfectly. Go at your own pace. If you struggle at any point, remember that moving slowly and completing the journey is more important than finishing it in forty days. Just do your best and adjust as needed.

3. *What if I am currently separated from my children?*

Get creative rather than giving up. Focus on doing what you can do. You can read the book, save up the dares, and then complete appropriate ones whenever opportunities arise during your limited moments of interaction. Or you may turn the dares into prayers for your child. Some are possible to complete through the mail or over the Internet. Simply adapt to your situation.

4. *What if my children do not respond well to this experience?*

This journey is more about your learning to love than how your child responds. Keep going. Most will respond positively right away while others will need more time. If there are years of pain and emotional damage between you, it will take greater nourishment and healing. Be patient, think long-term, and never underestimate the power of unconditional love.

5. *Should I do this for one child at a time or for all my children at the same time?*

You can do it either way. You can go through the forty days with each child, making it a special experience for them alone, but recognize that this will require more time. If you take this route, consider helping your other children understand what you're doing so they don't feel like you're playing favorites. Another option is to go through the journey together with all your kids, but pause on the days that require individual attention, and complete that dare with each child separately before moving on to the next dare. Do whatever works best for your context.

Our hope for each *Love Dare* book is that the adventure will add a fresh dose of the extraordinary to your relationships.

Then as you learn new things, be sure to share your story with others to inspire and encourage them in their journey! Don't you wish your parents had done this for you? Dare to love!

Blessings to you,

Stephen and Alex Kendrick
Authors, *The Love Dare for Parents*

As the Father loved Me,
I also have loved you;
abide in My love.

John 15:9 nkjv

WHERE ARE YOU AS A PARENT TODAY?
Free Assessment

Being a parent envelops so much of who you are, there's rarely time to step back and evaluate how you are doing and ensure you are loving your children the way you desire.

To help you gain a quick snapshot of your present parenting and to chart your progress throughout this *Love Dare* journey, we have developed a FREE, personalized parenting assessment that's simple, easy to access, and private for your use.

Simply go to **LoveDareTest.com**.

In just a few minutes, you can quickly discover your key areas of growth and identify how to more strategically use *The Love Dare for Parents* to benefit you. Your results come with helpful suggestions on a number of core categories that factor into overall parenting success. You will also be led back to specific "days" in *The Love Dare for Parents* that will speak most directly to your own needs. And you can return to freely take the test again and again, tracking your growth each time.

Created in partnership with LifeWay Research, one of today's leading developers of survey tools on cultural trends and issues involving faith and relationships, this unique parenting evaluation is sure to bless and inform you. Whether you take it alone, with your spouse, or even anonymously, we believe you'll find it extremely helpful toward your greatest days ever as a parent.

Be sure to also enjoy the FREE *Love Dare Marriage Evaluation* available at the same site. We all have a lot to learn . . . but the future is bright and hopeful with coming opportunities to love each other better and love our children well.

Now Let's Begin
Introduction

The Scriptures say that children are gifts from God. They are beautiful fruits of your life and priceless arrows in your quiver (Psalm 127:3–5). God makes them in His image, creates them with a purpose, loves them without limitation, and then places them in your care. They are both your inheritance and your legacy.

While your own parents are likely set in their ways, your children are still moldable. So even though to the world you may be just another common citizen, you can be to your son or daughter the hero of their story, the conqueror of their crisis, and the molder of their dreams. They are designed to daily discover from you their identity, worth, and values.

If we could somehow fully grasp how fast our kids will grow up and the value of every moment with them, we would be overwhelmed. Approximately 6,575 days pass between a child's birth and his or her eighteenth birthday. And though our parenting does not end there, moms and dads too often squander this priceless ocean of opportunities while chasing momentary pleasures and pennies in the sand.

This book will dare you to love and influence your children while you can. Your future can become a tapestry of experiences that introduce each of them to unselfish, unconditional love. Parenting is wonderful, difficult, and life-changing, and no one should have a greater impact on your children than you. So may God bless you as you begin this adventure.

But be sure of this: it will take courage and endurance. If you accept this dare, you must take the view that instead of *following* your heart, you are choosing to *lead* it. The Bible says that "the heart is more deceitful than all else" (Jeremiah 17:9), and it will always pursue that which feels right at the moment.

Instead of letting your emotions rule, this is a journey of exploring and demonstrating genuine love, even when your desire is dry and your motives are low. The truth is, love is a decision and not just a feeling. It is selfless, sacrificial, and transformational. And when love is truly demonstrated as it was intended, it results in greater enjoyment, more lasting influence, and a legacy with few regrets.

Like the original *Love Dare*, each day of this journey will contain three very important elements:

First, a unique aspect of love and parenting will be discussed. Read each day carefully and be open to a new understanding of what it means to genuinely express love to your children.

Second, you will be given a specific dare to do for your children. Some will be easy and some very challenging. But take each dare seriously, and be creative and courageous enough to attempt it. Don't be discouraged if outside circumstances prevent you from accomplishing a specific dare. Just pick back up as soon as you can and proceed with the journey.

Last, you will be given journal space to log what you are learning and doing, and how your child is responding. If you take advantage of this space to capture what is happening with both of you, these records should become priceless to you and your children in the future.

Don't give up and don't get discouraged. Resolve to courageously make it through to the end. Learning to truly love is one of the most important things you will ever do.

Now these three remain: faith, hope, and love.
But the greatest of these is love. (1 Corinthians 13:13 HCSB)

IF I SPEAK WITH THE TONGUES OF MEN AND
OF ANGELS, BUT DO NOT HAVE LOVE, I HAVE
BECOME A NOISY GONG OR A CLANGING CYMBAL.

IF I HAVE THE GIFT OF PROPHECY,
AND KNOW ALL MYSTERIES AND ALL
KNOWLEDGE; AND IF I HAVE ALL FAITH,
SO AS TO REMOVE MOUNTAINS,
BUT DO NOT HAVE LOVE, I AM NOTHING.

AND IF I GIVE ALL MY POSSESSIONS TO
FEED THE POOR, AND IF I SURRENDER MY
BODY TO BE BURNED, BUT DO NOT HAVE LOVE,
IT PROFITS ME NOTHING.

1 CORINTHIANS 13:1–3

DAY 1
Love blooms

. . . you, being rooted and grounded in love . . . (Ephesians 3:17)

Love is life's purest and most powerful motivator. It
always does what is best for others and invites us to reach
new heights in our relationships. Love brings fresh flavor to
our living and renewed joy to our giving. Every relationship
becomes more meaningful with it. No family is truly happy
without it.

For this reason, love creates the richest soil in which to raise
children. As flowers in a greenhouse are supplied with an ideal
environment for growth, so a home filled with love provides
the best context for children to flourish. Your kids should not
only be the fruit of your love, but should also be deeply rooted
in the nurture of your love . . . on a daily basis.

Every child is born with a lifelong thirst for love. Their
hearts desperately need it like their little lungs need oxygen.
It fills and energizes them. It stabilizes and secures them.
Sons who grow up in loving families tend to stand taller in the
day and sleep deeper in the night. Daughters rooted in love
are more radiant when they rise and less fearful if they fail.
Successes are amplified with celebration. Failures are minimized with tender consolation.

The love you express to your children is infinitely more
valuable than any possession you could give them. You can
educate them in prestigious schools, dress them in the finest
clothes, guide them with the wisest rules, and boldly confront
their worst fears. But if they do not rest in your unconditional
love, you are neglecting a much more vital need for their true
success in life.

Children come prepackaged with core questions hidden in their hearts: *Do I matter? Does anyone truly care about me? Do I have what it takes?* Dads and moms are commissioned to be God's first responders to answer these questions clearly and repeatedly over the years.

When kids are unsure if the words "I love you" apply to their hearts, they will be constantly tempted to pursue validation in their performance or in the opinions of others. Insecurities will abound. Failure will become more devastating because their sense of self-worth and identity hangs in the balance.

But what happens when a child is deeply loved by his parents over the years? His needs are more consistently met. Her dreams are faithfully encouraged. He enjoys their understanding. She is welcomed with their affection. Children like these receive instruction and protection. They're disciplined and accepted. They're assured of your patience and forgiveness, and free to share their hearts honestly without fear of overreaction. They'll even weather intense seasons of disappointment with the stability your love supplies.

What's more, when this kind of loving relationship develops between you and your child, it becomes the best environment for you to pass on your beliefs, values, faith, and heritage to them and to future generations.

Love creates a safe zone to deal with life's lessons and harsh realities. Rebuke and discipline are more palatable when seasoned with genuine love. Your children will be more likely to discern and reject the lies of others if they first receive your wise counsel within the environment of your tender affection.

The Scriptures illustrate this reality by saying to us, "We are no longer to be children, tossed here and there by waves and carried about by every wind of doctrine, by the trickery of men, by craftiness in deceitful scheming; but speaking the truth in love, we are to grow up in all aspects" (Ephesians 4:14–15).

Though these verses are speaking of spiritual growth within the church, the power of "speaking the truth in love" is also fundamental to effective parenting—to *any* relationship for that matter. Truth guides what you say while love guides how, why, and when you say it. When love is the fertile soil, truth becomes a more fruitful seed.

By working together, truth and love build deep trust between you and your child. In contrast, when parents force truth into a relationship that's poisoned with anger, bitterness, insecurity, or emotional isolation, those truths tend to become twisted or rejected over time. Pain and misunderstanding become silent weeds that can choke out what you're trying to communicate. Even when you speak clearly, your wise words may fall on toxic soil. This is why past hurts must always be uncovered and dealt with compassionately to gain a child's heart and ear again.

Test yourself with these questions:

• How loving and fertile is the soil in our home?
• How much love do my children sense from me each day?
• Do the truths I share take root? Or are they ignored?
• What toxins or weeds need to be eliminated?

You may have grown up in a very loving home, and the idea of freely pouring out love on your children may come easily and naturally. Or you may have always felt a deep void of love at home, and now you long to provide what was never modeled or shared with you. In either case, we challenge you to resolve that you will be committed to establishing a strong environment of love for your children to bloom within. Purpose to begin this today.

WORDS ARE A POWERFUL WAY TO
COMMUNICATE LOVE. THE FIRST DARE
IS SIMPLY TO FIND A MOMENT WHEN YOU
CAN VERBALLY EXPRESS LOVE TO YOUR
CHILDREN. WHETHER THEY ARE IN YOUR
HOUSE OR REACHABLE BY PHONE, IF IT IS
POSSIBLE, MAKE SURE THEY HEAR YOU
SAY THE WORDS "I LOVE YOU" TODAY.

___ Check here when you've completed today's dare.

What was the result of your interaction? Did they respond?
Was this easy or difficult for you? Why are these simple words,
though often taken for granted, so very important to say
consistently?

_____

_____

_____

_____

_____

_____

_____

_____

_____

This is My commandment, that you love one another. (John 15:12)

DAY 2
Love is patient

Fathers, do not provoke your children to anger, but bring them up in the discipline and instruction of the Lord. (Ephesians 6:4)

When you truly love someone, two key attributes will show up on a regular basis: patience and kindness. In fact, many other characteristics of love are based upon these two attributes. *Patience* is how love diffuses something negative; *kindness* is how love initiates something positive. One takes in a deep breath; the other breathes out life. As you know, raising a child requires an unlimited supply of both. But today, we will focus on the first of these two essentials . . . *patience*.

Patience is when love chooses to "suffer long" for the greater good of another. It is like an experienced farmer who knows that fruitful fields only come if he is willing to endure the heat of the sun. Patience is like a wise builder who spends long hours slaving over blueprints, negotiating contracts, and overseeing supplies so his desired vision can become a reality. Both the farmer and the builder must persist when they want to resist. They must daily keep investing time and hard effort until they can celebrate the great harvest or the open house.

Likewise, being a loving parent requires a long supply of this amazing attribute. You are cultivating and building up your children, and all your work and sacrifice will ultimately pay off. But today requires your enduring patience. It is something we all need but rarely delight in demonstrating. Yet love invites us to exercise it frequently as parents. And when we do, it brings maturity both to us and our children, as well as needed grace and peace in the midst of our problems.

Children have an amazing ability to test the level of their parents' patience by their tone, disobedience, irresponsibility, or any lack of respect. Sometimes parents can feel so angry, they say or do things in the heat of emotion that damage young hearts and minds. The impact can leave a deep and lasting emotional scar for many years to come.

This is why we find God's patience so exemplary. When Moses was on the mountaintop, he discovered why God kept putting up with His rebellious, complaining children: God was "compassionate and gracious, slow to anger, and abounding in lovingkindness" (Exodus 34:6). He let His overflowing love control His anger. Whenever He did choose to be angry and firm, it was only after multiple, extended demonstrations of His compassion and patience.

Today, God is still gracious and patient with us as His children. So when we are unlovable and selfish, distracted and disobedient, we need to remember His enduring love for us and let His example of love overflow onto us and our children.

We must refuse to spring off the handle in front of our offspring. When they see us controlling our anger, it teaches them to control theirs. The Scripture says, "Be angry, and yet do not sin" (Ephesians 4:26). Sometimes anger is appropriate, but we should never let it get out of bounds. Discipline and correction must be wisely rationed, but only after we've first demonstrated loving patience.

Do your children see you as an angry, frustrated parent? Or would they describe you as compassionate and patient instead? Love chooses restraint. It controls your emotions rather than letting them control you. It challenges you to develop a long fuse instead of igniting a short temper. If you unnecessarily blow your top, it reminds you to humble yourself and quickly apologize, knowing much is at stake.

Wrath, on the other hand, is cruel (Proverbs 27:4). It divides and isolates. It weakens us and wounds others. It causes us to behave in foolish, regrettable ways. It almost never makes things better and usually generates additional problems.

If you struggle with anger, ask yourself why. Are your expectations realistic? Are you angry with somebody else, yet taking it out on your kids? You may harbor painful memories of a parent's harsh anger toward you when you were young. But this pain doesn't need to be passed on to your children.

Sometimes anger is rooted in our own sin or hypocrisy. We often get the most angry with our kids in the same areas where we ourselves are weak. But overreacting to wrongful actions and attitudes that are familiar to us doesn't do anything to "fix" us, and it only frustrates them. That's where a humble confession may yield more effective instruction than the firm anger of your correction. When they know you love them and can admit your own humanity, your counsel and training carry much more meaning.

Patience is always welcome. It gives people more time to work through their issues. It beautifully diffuses conflict before trouble has a chance to escalate. It whispers peace into situations brewing toward eruption. It's not a blanket form of tolerance that lets everything go, but rather a wise surveyor of the situation, allowing proper steps to be taken.

Parenting does call for action against carelessness and defiance. But we must differentiate between true rebellion and what might be childish ignorance. Our kids don't think like us; why do we expect them to act like us? We must factor in the circumstances, their age, and their level of maturity.

So instead of rising up and tearing down, let love *calm* you down. Then you can build them up. The more patient you are today, the more victories you can celebrate tomorrow.

TODAY'S DARE

Write the words "Love Is Patient" on a piece of paper and temporarily tape it to your mirror or refrigerator. When you see it over the next few weeks, purpose to display patience throughout the day as a further demonstration of your love to your children.

___ Check here when you've completed today's dare.

Did any past instances come to mind when you could have demonstrated more patience? What happened today that gave you an opportunity to show patience?

The farmer waits for the precious produce of the soil, being patient. (James 5:7)

Day 3
Love is kind

Be kind to one another, tender-hearted, forgiving each other,
just as God in Christ also has forgiven you. (Ephesians 4:32)

One of the greatest expressions of genuine love is showing kindness to your children. Kindness is the sweet aroma they should notice whenever your love enters the room. It inspires us to care for them. It flavors how we treat them. Whereas patience is love minimizing the negative, kindness is love initiating the positive. Patience helps us avoid problems, while kindness helps us be a blessing.

Love will make you kind, and kindness will make you likable. When you are kind to your children, they will enjoy being around you. In fact, it gives you favor in all your relationships and opens doors for your children.

"Do not let kindness and truth leave you," the Bible says. "Bind them around your neck, write them on the tablet of your heart. So you will find favor and good repute in the sight of God and man" (Proverbs 3:3–4).

Kindness is love in action. It rejects passivity and reaches out. It takes time to listen, then takes steps to help. It never requires the easiest path or simplest method to engage in the lives of others.

Specifically, kindness leads to *service*—seeing a need and moving to meet it—honoring others by putting their interests ahead of your own, even in little things. At home with your children, you can model kindness by serving them without complaining, as well as quickly pointing out and celebrating moments when they show kindness themselves.

Scripture describes the kindness of God by how He freely extends grace to His children, giving them exactly what they need (Ephesians 2:6–9). And He commands us to follow His lead by consistently being kind to others (Ephesians 4:32). This should begin with those in our own families.

Kindness also brings *willingness*. It makes us cooperative, more ready to say "yes" than "no" to a request. It helps us become more agreeable and seek unity rather than coming up with another reason to dig in our heels. It teaches us to release and give rather than resist and hold back.

Kindness likewise seasons all our interactions with *gentleness*. It makes us more sensitive and tenderhearted. It stamps "Handle with Care" on the hearts of those with whom we come into contact and avoids being unnecessarily harsh or insensitive in our tone of voice or choice of words. Consider this thought: Just about everything we say or do could probably be greatly enhanced with the addition of a little more kindness.

Why is this important? Because if we are not careful as parents, we too can become very unkind to the little ones we love. It is so easy to think that because we are the parent, because we are so much more mature and have sacrificed so much for our kids, we can act however we want around them. Didn't we change their diapers? Haven't we spent untold dollars on them and put up with years of their runny noses and misbehavior? Yes. But love reminds us that our sacrifices never give us license to be uncaring or harsh.

Fathers should display more kindness than other men their children are around. This is what their kids are longing to experience (Proverbs 19:22). Mothers should have words of kindness flowing from their lips (Proverbs 31:26).

Be honest: Do your children see you as someone who is consistently kind to them and others? Do you model kindness in how you speak about people behind their backs? Do you give, share, and reach out to those in need? Do you regularly take the initiative to show kindness?

Your kids are more sensitive to you than almost anyone on earth. When you resist or ignore them, they will struggle inside and likely not respond to you well. But when you create an environment of tender love and kindness, they become more open to sharing their heart with you and listening to the words you say and the lessons you share.

Love leads you to look for opportunities to show kindness to your kids. This doesn't mean *doing* everything for them. Rather, it's the fine balance between loving them well and teaching them to love others. Part of their becoming an effective parent or leader as an adult is in developing the heart of a servant as a youth—the heart they should see in you.

So teach them to practice kindness around you and their siblings as well. Give them opportunities to serve at meals and take care of one another's needs at home. When they're ready, take them to places where serving others will build an appetite and heart for ministry. Visit a home for the elderly or a struggling neighbor who would be thrilled to receive a home cooked meal for no other reason than kindness. Help them mow a lawn for a widow or reach out to children who have no father at home. These experiences remind your kids how precious and important other people are in the eyes of God, and that our kindness honors Him and reflects His character.

As you show and encourage kindness in your children, you are investing in the type of heart God calls us to nurture. It's the Golden Rule: treating others the way you want to be treated, freely giving the very thing we long to receive from those with whom we live every day. It's the blessing of kindness. And that's the beauty of how true love takes action.

TODAY'S DARE

SURPRISE YOUR CHILDREN TODAY BY DOING SOME UNEXPECTED ACT OF KINDNESS. AS THEY TAKE NOTE OF YOUR GESTURE, ASK THEM TO DO SOMETHING KIND FOR SOMEONE ELSE THAT IS ALSO UNEXPECTED.

___ Check here when you've completed today's dare.

What did you choose to do for them as an act of kindness? How did they respond? What did they do for someone else in return?

_____

_____

_____

_____

_____

_____

_____

_____

_____

Sow with a view to righteousness, reap in accordance with kindness. (Hosea 10:12)

DAY 4
Love values

Behold, children are a gift of the LORD. (Psalm 127:3)

The world often sends a message that children are a burden and an inconvenience. They cost a lot of money and take up valuable time. They get in your way. They disobey. They whine.

As a result, many people avoid having them. They chase money, success, pleasure, and possessions instead. And if they do dare to bear children, they're warned to limit themselves to one or maybe two . . . at the most.

But when a child finally arrives and joins a family, something changes. She steals your heart and changes your life. He introduces daily wonder and adventure. What you were once content without, you now cannot *live* without. You would die for them. Your greatest fear becomes losing them.

Then—ironically—the world that once discouraged children now eagerly wants their attention. They constantly advertise for them to watch their programs, use their lingo, and buy their products. They recruit them to attend their events and work at their jobs. They beg them to serve their causes, vote for their candidates, and fight for their agendas.

That's why we need to listen to the consistent counsel of genuine love rather than the shifting opinions of a self-centered culture. Love reminds us that children are and have always been priceless, desirable, and a unique treasure. They are our walking, living legacies, each of them bearing untapped potential beyond measure. Love helps us view them the way God views them—as one of our greatest blessings in life. A sacred trust. A privileged responsibility. A precious delight.

A common thread runs throughout the pages of Scripture: God's great love for children. The first command He gives in the Bible is to "be fruitful and multiply" (Genesis 1:28). The first time love is mentioned in the Bible, God speaks of it in reference to the deep love Abraham had for his son Isaac (Genesis 22:2). God's covenant blessings upon the patriarchs primarily involved the promise of children and how future nations would rise and be blessed through them (Genesis 26:1–4). He asked families to dedicate their firstborn as a gift back to Him (Exodus 13:2). The last verse in the Old Testament explains God's desire to turn the hearts of fathers back to their children (Malachi 4:6).

And perhaps most descriptive of all: "Behold, children are a gift of the LORD, the fruit of the womb is a reward. Like arrows in the hand of a warrior, so are the children of one's youth" (Psalm 127:3–4).

This word *gift* means an inheritance given by God, presented as part of one's allotted portion in life (Isaiah 54:17). Children are like precious fruit in the orchard, a cherished reward to savor and enjoy, worth all the work invested by the farmer. They are like prized, life-preserving arrows in the hand of a warrior, uniquely formed to be launched out, making a powerful impact on the world. Consider how, contrary to common thinking, each of these analogies—inheritance, fruit, arrows—refers to things people usually want more of, not something they wish to avoid or minimize.

Jesus rebuked His followers for treating children as an unwanted intrusion or irritation. Instead, He invited the children closer, saying that great blessing comes from welcoming them into our lives, "for the kingdom of God belongs to such as these" (Mark 10:14). He placed a little boy in front of His disciples and said, "Whoever then humbles himself as this child, he is the greatest in the kingdom of heaven. And whoever receives one such child in My name receives Me" (Matthew 18:4–5).

Children are also given to us to help us personally mature as parents. They teach us how to stop being so selfish and to give sacrificially. They pull us out of our comfort zones and stretch our abilities. They repeat our words and test our integrity. They expose our pride and deepen our humility. They help us learn to love more willingly. They enter this world as if to say, "Here I am, a mirror to reveal you, ready clay for you to mold. I am given to bear your name and reflect your likeness. I am more valuable than anything you own, and I could become your greatest investment in the world."

But beyond this, children also enrich the flavor of every season of our lives. Your money will never love you back, kiss you at night, or run in and celebrate with you on Christmas morning. Your possessions will never walk with you down the aisle, give you grandchildren, cry at your funeral, or carry on your legacy to future generations.

So regardless of how old your children are, dare to set your eyes and heart back upon them. To prize them. To follow the example of Jesus, welcoming them into your arms and lovingly blessing them and their future lives (Mark 10:16).

As deeply loved by God.

As deeply loved by you.

Are they lots of work? Yes. Do they continually cost us money? Yes. Can they rebel and be sources of great stress? Yes. But are they irreplaceable and priceless beyond measure? Are they worth the investment of your life, your love, your time, and your attention? Absolutely, a million times over.

They are wrapped by divine hands and presented in love. They are the fruit of your life and God's living reward.

TODAY'S DARE

COMMUNICATE TO YOUR CHILDREN TODAY
THAT THEY ARE A TREASURE TO YOU. SAY IN
YOUR OWN WORDS, "YOU ARE A PRICELESS GIFT
TO ME, AND I AM GRATEFUL THAT YOU ARE IN
MY LIFE." THEN THANK GOD FOR THEM AND
FOR THE CHANCE HE HAS GIVEN YOU
TO DAILY LOVE AND VALUE THEM.

___ Check here when you've completed today's dare.

Do you tend to view your children as a burden of life or a blessing from God? How do you need to change your view of them? What did you say to them today?

_____

_____

_____

_____

_____

_____

_____

_____

_____

_____

_____

_____

Here I am with the children God gave me. (Hebrews 2:13 HCSB)

DAY 5
Love is wonderful

Such knowledge is too wonderful for me;
it is too high, I cannot attain to it. (Psalm 139:6)

Every child is a one of a kind mini-masterpiece. No known duplicates exist. They each have distinctive fingerprints, heart rhythms, eye patterns, and blood constitution. Even identical twins can be physically alike and yet light years apart in how they are mentally wired and gifted. Our children do not just *grow up* different; they *show up* different.

Though circumstances and training will greatly affect their lives, the originality that is already ingrained into each of our children reflects brilliant preplanning. Every birthmark is a trademark. Every special feature is a signature of divine design.

The Scriptures state that God is not only the One who opens a mother's womb to conceive (Genesis 30:22), but He personally gets involved forming and weaving the systems of a child's body into a tapestry of life (Psalm 139:13–14). He draws the blueprints for every little boy and owns the copyright on every little girl.

But His handiwork goes far beyond gender, shoe size, and eye color. His genius also inscribes the intricacies of their personalities. Their perks and quirks and the bounces in their gait. Their eagerness to jump or their cautious tendency to wait. He handpicks their preferences. He rations out their healthy passions.

But these are not random choices. God is always intentional as to why He makes each child the way He does. He desires His power, creativity, and image to be uniquely reflected in each living soul. Even in His allowance of unexpected birth defects, His conclusions are kind (John 9:1–3). His strength is often revealed most vividly through human weakness, cultivating deeper character and compassion in their families.

Your children are also distinctively prepared for the purpose of helping others (Ephesians 2:10). He places them into a specific time and space and enables them to thrive where others are ill-equipped, to meet unique needs others cannot.

So when you consider the wonder of each of your children, love invites you as a parent to go on an adventure of discovery by unpacking the marvelous mystery of their design.

It is good to ask: *How are they wired? How are they unique? Who are they becoming? What is already in them that needs to be discovered and inspired?*

You may already recognize that their gender and birth order are gifts, not accidents. Sons and daughters will not need the same training. He needs masculine adventure, cultivation of inner courage, and training for responsible manhood. She needs to be lovingly affirmed in her beauty, strengthened within her femininity, and directed in how to connect with others unselfishly.

Your firstborn child may relate better to adults and lead others well, but needs to learn not to always have his own way. The second-born may be more competitive, the youngest more independent, but each must be directed to channel their drives for good.

Have you discerned what type of intelligence your child has? Some kids can remember words and facts easily while others are capable entrepreneurs. One may be a natural engineer while another is a master of friendship and resolves relationship problems with ease. Some are meticulously technical; others are cleverly comical. Each one will shine in some way and should be encouraged and valued for the brilliance within their mentality.

Let your kindness also uncover how your children best communicate and receive love. Each one should be loved the same amount, but not in the same way. One may most desire your physical affection, while another primarily needs your focused time. See if your son or daughter is energized more when praised, served, or receiving a gift of some kind. As you discover what helps them feel the most fulfilled, you can then strategically focus your attention and energy more effectively with each one when you are with them.

Loving parenting requires discovery with direction. It's listening and learning how a child thinks, dreams, and grows. It's separating their God-given leaning from their temporary longing. It's watching their habits, guarding them against their weaknesses, and growing them in their strengths.

Too often parents misunderstand and misguide. Or they preplan too rigidly and then force and frustrate their child to become something God never intended. If your tiny daughter thrives at the piano, don't pressure her to tackle your tuba. If your son thrives at writing and singing, don't belittle him for not being an all-star quarterback. Instead, uncover and embrace the treasure you have been given. Accept and affirm their design. Water and cultivate the seeds God has already planted.

Then instead of chasing someone else's dreams, they can mature and be secure in their own. And by your guidance and focused love, they can joyfully echo the words of the psalmist when he gratefully prayed, "You formed my inward parts; You wove me in my mother's womb. I will give thanks to You, for I am fearfully and wonderfully made; wonderful are Your works, and my soul knows it very well" (Psalm 139:13–14).

THANK GOD FOR HOW HE DESIGNED YOUR
CHILDREN, AND THEN DISCERN IF EACH ONE
RESPONDS BEST TO PHYSICAL AFFECTION,
VERBAL AFFIRMATION, SPENDING QUALITY
TIME TOGETHER, GIVING A GIFT, OR SERVING
A NEED OF THEIRS. IF YOU KNOW THEIR PRE-
FERRED WAY TO GIVE AND RECEIVE LOVE, TAKE
A FEW MOMENTS TO COMMUNICATE LOVE TO
THEM IN THAT WAY BEFORE THE DAY ENDS.

___ Check here when you've completed today's dare.

What strengths do you recognize in each of your children, and
how can you show your gratitude for how God designed them?
If you are not sure how they best prefer to give and receive
love, then consider what they ask for the most and complain
about when they don't receive. How did you choose to show
love to them today? How did they respond?

_____

_____

_____

_____

_____

Your hands made me and fashioned me . . .
that I may learn Your commandments. (Psalm 119:73)

DAY 6
Love is not selfish

Do nothing from selfishness or empty conceit, but with humility of mind regard one another as more important than yourselves. (Philippians 2:3)

Children are God's homework assignment to parents. We are commissioned to love, teach, and train them up for successful adulthood. But this process requires so much careful focus and attention, a father or mother must daily set aside something very specific that will otherwise stand in the way: *their own selfishness.*

Selfishness is like a disease that suffocates our capacity to love. While love asks us to deny ourselves for the sake of another, selfishness demands we put ourselves first at their expense. When we choose to be self-centered, we become less kind and content—more needy, sensitive, and demanding. More unsatisfiable. Moodiness and impatience, laziness and irresponsibility, are only selfishness in disguise.

And we all struggle with it. We despise this trait in others but justify it in ourselves. Almost every wrong and sinful action can be traced back to a selfish motive.

Love, however, "does not seek its own" (1 Corinthians 13:5). It finds satisfaction in bringing kindness, health, and blessing to others. Loving parents are bent on taking good care of the flawed little humans with whom they share their lives.

Unselfish people make amazing friends, spouses, and parents. They are willing to table their own demands and lose themselves in the joy of loving, giving, and serving. The more we each learn to daily turn away from our own selfishness, the stronger, more lovable, and fulfilled we can become.

Society teaches us to focus on our personal feelings and desires as the highest priority. But children show up constantly needing feeding, cleaning, and leading, which requires a lot of work on our part. They cry when we want quiet, start wars with one another when we want peace, and can knock on the locked door of our bedroom at the most inopportune times.

Parents can zero in on the weight of these responsibilities as something that limits their ability to do whatever they want whenever they want. But what our children *actually* do is uniquely reveal our selfishness in living color and invite us to live outside of its constant demands.

This is really one of the uncommon purposes of parenting. God strategically uses our children to help us become less self-centered, less self-absorbed, and more loving . . . like Him. He stretches and matures us with plenty of opportunities to deny ourselves and demonstrate sacrificial love and patience toward our children. Just like He does for us.

But in guarding against being selfish *around* our children, we must also try not to be selfish *for* our children. Ultimately, our children belong to God even more than they belong to us. And the most loving thing we can do is to willingly dedicate them back to Him, guarding against putting our desires for them or their desires for themselves above *God's* desires.

The biblical story of Hannah (1 Samuel 1–2) gives us a wonderful picture of how to wisely view our children. Unable to have a child of her own, she humbly prayed and petitioned the Lord with all her heart, and He blessed her with Samuel. Out of gratefulness, Hannah unselfishly dedicated her beloved son back to the Lord, and God used him in mighty ways to bless their nation and counsel its future kings.

In the Gospel of Luke, we see Mary and Joseph dedicating Jesus in the temple (Luke 2:22), then consistently honoring God with how they parented Him over the years, recognizing Him as belonging to His heavenly Father.

You, too, are a steward of the children God has entrusted to you. As a steward, you resolve to take full responsibility for their nurture, training, and care—to dedicate them to the Lord and to purpose in your heart to raise them with God's help and grace. You must refuse to let your selfishness get in the way of what God has called you to do. Otherwise, you will tend to treat them as an irritation, worry about them like another possession, or worship them as an idol.

But when you recognize that God owns them and has made you the loving steward of them, then you can fully enjoy them as God's treasure to be taken care of and offered back to Him. Parents who put their kids first or build their identity around them face a much harder time letting them go. Then those parents are more apt to struggle with their own sense of identity and value after their kids are gone.

We must remember that selfishness and love are in constant opposition to one another. You can't be acting out of real love and selfishness at the same time. Selfishness causes us to put our own hobbies, entertainment, and comfort above the needs of our children. It leads many parents to refuse to have more children because they don't want anything to stretch them further beyond themselves.

Choosing to love your children will cause you to say "no" to what you want so you can say "yes" to what they need. It doesn't mean you cannot enjoy personal fulfillment, but you don't negate their welfare and needs just so you can enjoy your own. Love instead fights for what is best in God's eyes with a heart of gratitude. We should thank God for granting us the daily opportunity to love our children unselfishly and to grow stronger, wiser, and more Christlike in the process.

TAKE SOME TIME IN PRAYER TO IDENTIFY
AND PUSH ASIDE ANY HURDLES OF
SELFISHNESS IN YOUR OWN LIFE THAT
MAY BE KEEPING YOU FROM LOVING YOUR
CHILDREN MORE EFFECTIVELY. THEN
PURPOSE TO DEDICATE YOUR CHILDREN
TO THE LORD AS A GIFT BACK TO HIM.

___ Check here when you've completed today's dare.

What did God reveal to you when you prayed? What did
He prompt you to do? How do you think your children will
respond to this change in you?

I rejoice in my sufferings for your sake. (Colossians 1:24)

DAY 7
Love is not irritable

Put on a heart of compassion, kindness, humility, gentleness and
patience; bearing with one another. (Colossians 3:12–13)

Love is a calming breeze, not a storm waiting to happen.
Your first response to problems either leaves your kids with
refreshing and positive character lessons or with painful
memories of how *not* to behave under pressure.

To be irritable means "to be near the point of a knife." On
edge. Never far from being poked. Sadly, some parents never
pass up an opportunity to get upset with their children. They feel
obligated to take full advantage of anything that goes wrong by
expressing how deeply frustrated they are with the situation.

But let's be honest. No one likes to cuddle with a porcupine
or lie down in a briar patch. And these shouldn't be the only
options we give our children inside their own home. If we
immediately voice irritation rather than tempering emotion,
we not only make ourselves taste the bitterness in our hearts
but force-feed it to everyone else around us as well.

Love is hard to offend and quick to forgive. It doesn't act
like a martyr over minor mishaps. It asks us to extend a touch-
ing response, not a touchy reaction. And it calls us to quickly
defuse any explosion that irritability wants to set off.

According to 1 Corinthians 13:5, love is not easily "pro-
voked." It isn't moody, crabby, or harmfully sarcastic. Rather,
it extends the same loving patience to our children that God
grants to us, demonstrating righteous anger only when appropriate, and only then for short periods of time.

When we are grumpy at home, we are displaying the opposite of what love is calling us to do. Our children will never be

perfect, so why do we act surprised when they make mistakes? We are not perfect before God, yet He doesn't strike us with lightning when we fail. Instead He demonstrates patience with us while compelling us to get things right with Him (2 Peter 3:9). Likewise, parental correction and discipline should never spring from uncontrolled anger or from using our children as the easy target to release our own tension.

If your kids always sense your unearned irritation, you will cause them to feel less loved and more insecure. You will unintentionally push their hearts away from yours. And if this tendency continues over time, they will likely adopt it as their expression of choice later on to their own children, thereby continuing a harmful pattern for generations to come.

That's why fighting off the root causes of irritation is like kicking harmful intruders out of your home. Don't even let them in. Determine to no longer let minor problems produce major reactions. Resolve to exercise emotional self-control. Choose to guard your words when frustration starts to well up inside of you, and let love direct the manner of your expressions, actions, and even your countenance.

Irritability usually flows from two bitter springs: *stress* and *selfishness*. When you react to your children, ask yourself if your stress level is actually being caused by factors already at play inside you rather than whatever your kids are currently doing. If you are under stress from other relationships, your health, or your finances, these may be draining you and weakening your ability to be self-controlled and kind.

Are you overworking, overspending, or struggling with anger in another area? Are you lacking rest, exercise, or nutrition? Is a spiritual deficiency depleting your heart and soul?

Remember, life is more a marathon than a sprint, so you must pace yourself and prioritize. Your relationship with God, your marriage, and your children must always remain the top priorities. This means protecting your time with them and fighting to prevent anything from taking your love and devotion away from them and toward secondary things.

Let the Word of God lead you to relate more graciously with others (Colossians 3:12–14). To pray through your anxieties (Philippians 4:6–7). To guard you from overworking by reminding you to take a Sabbath day to rest, worship, and refocus each week (Exodus 20:8–11). This pattern strategically allows you time to recharge and add margin or breathing room to your weekly schedule.

Irritation can also come from selfishness in our hearts. Lust, bitterness, greed, and pride are never satisfied and always cause restlessness and anger. But love inspires us to quit focusing on ourselves and let go of these harmful and unnecessary motivations.

Love brings freedom by leading you to forgive instead of holding a grudge. To be grateful instead of greedy. To prioritize your family rather than sacrifice them for a promotion at work. In each decision, love ultimately lowers your stress and sets up your heart to respond to your children with patience and encouragement rather than anger and exasperation.

Run a mental checklist, and you just may discover a hidden reason why your irritation level is higher than it should be. Bring that area before God, and genuinely ask Him to forgive you and help you. When we truly turn to Him, acknowledging our faults, His strong and gentle Spirit brings peace, comfort, and wisdom into our frustrating circumstances, and His Word gives us insight so we can be more like Him and bring direction and life to those we love the most.

TODAY'S DARE

CHOOSE TODAY TO START REACTING TO
YOUR CHILDREN WITH LOVE INSTEAD OF
IRRITATION. BEGIN BY MAKING A LIST OF
AREAS WHERE YOU NEED TO LOWER STRESS
IN YOUR LIFE. THEN LIST ANY WRONG
MOTIVATIONS THAT YOU NEED TO
RELEASE FROM YOUR HEART.

___ Check here when you've completed today's dare.

Where do you need to release stress in your life? When have
you recently overreacted? What was your real motivation
behind it? What new decisions have you made today?

_____

_____

_____

_____

_____

_____

_____

_____

_____

_____

_____

_____

He who restrains his words has knowledge, and he who
has a cool spirit is a man of understanding. (Proverbs 17:27)

DAY 8
Love wins hearts

He will turn the hearts of the fathers to the children,
and the hearts of the children to their fathers. (Malachi 4:6 KJV)

Whoever has your children's hearts has their ears and significantly influences the direction of their lives. You can be the most spiritual, intelligent parent on the planet, but if you lose your children's hearts, they will likely turn away from you in the long run. Your ultimate effectiveness as a parent greatly depends upon this one key issue.

King David was a man after God's own heart, a great warrior, a successful leader, and a loving friend. But he lost the heart of his own son Absalom, and it resulted in painful family dysfunction, public shame, and the deaths of 20,000 men in battle (2 Samuel 13–18). How could this happen?

The fracture began when David grew distant in his own private walk with God and began hiding in sin. Absalom then watched David neglect to bring justice to his own son Amnon, who raped David's daughter Tamar, Absalom's sister. When Absalom tried to reengage with his father, he gained little traction and was turned away. So in revenge he killed the man who had hurt Tamar, but David neither rebuked or reached out to his wayward son. After Absalom finally returned home as a prodigal, he begged for David's attention but was ignored. The unresolved hurt and anger eventually led him to initiate a civil war against his own father. Absalom was killed in battle, leaving the broken relationship to haunt David forever.

After Absalom's death, David crowned his son Solomon to succeed him as king. And Solomon, having witnessed the tragic relationship between his father and half-brother, made an insightful request to his own child: "Give me your heart, my son, and let your eyes delight in my ways" (Proverbs 23:26). He knew what could happen if he didn't.

Solomon's request echoes through time to inspire and challenge us as parents today. Winning your children's hearts does not mean cowering, obeying their every wish, or giving them whatever they want. It means providing them the loving attention, affection, and affirmation they need while carefully guarding against any emotional distance, hurts, or unresolved issues from coming between you.

God puts a longing within all children when they are young to gain the attention and approval of their parents (Proverbs 4:1–4; 17:6). He also instructs fathers, saying, "Do not exasperate your children, so that they will not lose heart" (Colossians 3:21). We can win many battles in life but still lose the war at home if our children withdraw, rebel, and ignore us.

You can tell when children have turned their hearts away from their parents. The ongoing tones of disrespect. The lack of tenderness. Emotional distance. They have little desire to be near you or listen to you. Their words and attitudes reveal the hurt and anger brewing below the surface.

Children can emotionally pull away for many reasons. It could be your lack of time, attention, or tender affection. Broken promises. Your actions may communicate, "You're not really important enough for me to prioritize or care about what's going on in your life."

It could be the hard lines you've drawn. If they believe your discipline is too harsh, your demands are too great, or that you are playing favorites, a warning light will go off in their hearts. This can plant seeds of anger and resistance that later spring up into bitterness against you.

Training, discipline, and boundaries are necessary for good parenting, but they must be packaged and cushioned within a context of love. Sometimes appropriate words of rebuke can be unknowingly wrapped in a crushing tone or hateful facial expression. So parents should constantly be guided by the question, "How can I speak and handle my children in this situation without losing their hearts?"

Ask yourself:

- Do I have my children's hearts right now?
- Do they know they have mine?
- Do they care what I think?
- Do they want to spend time with me?
- Are they grieved when I am displeased?
- Are they loyal when I'm not watching?

The heart of your child is really at the heart of your parenting. If you realize you've lost one or more of your children's hearts, then quickly press pause on your schedule and ask God to help you draw them back to you.

But don't try to change your child before examining yourself first (Matthew 7:5). Ask if your heavenly Father currently has *your* heart? Are you loyal to Him and submitted to Him? If not, don't be surprised if your kids have been following your example by pulling their hearts away from you and from God.

Reach out to your children and ask, "Have I hurt you or wronged you in any way? Are you angry with me? How can I make it right? Help me understand what's going on inside you."

Be ready to listen, apologize, and help them work through their frustrations until all issues have been resolved. Let your love encourage you to make the necessary sacrifices, fulfill the promises, and do whatever it takes to make sure you have your children's hearts again.

TODAY'S DARE

REACH OUT TO YOUR CHILDREN ONE
BY ONE AND TELL THEM YOU WANT TO BE
CLOSER TO THEM THAN YOU ARE RIGHT NOW.
ASK THEM THE QUESTIONS MENTIONED
NEAR THE END OF TODAY'S CHAPTER, AND BE-
GIN TAKING STEPS TOWARD WINNING
AND KEEPING THEIR HEARTS.

___ Check here when you've completed today's dare.

If one or more of your children are resisting relationship with you right now, what have you concluded the reasons to be? On the other hand, what things are proving the most helpful in maintaining healthy access to their hearts? How could you keep doing more of it? What did you learn from talking with your kids individually about this?

_____

_____

_____

_____

_____

_____

_____

My son, if your heart is wise, my own heart also will be glad. (Proverbs 23:15)

DAY 9
Love cherishes

As one whom his mother comforts,
so I will comfort you. (Isaiah 66:13)

Men can love their children in deep, aspiring ways. Anyone who thinks a father's love is limited simply because he is male is reading more into stereotype than into reality or the richness of Scripture.

But still, priceless and precious is a mother's love. There is a reason why Mother's Day is the #1 card-sending holiday of the year. Why more people dine out on that one Sunday than on any other special occasion. God has made the love of a mother to be warm and wonderful.

When David looked for a word picture to describe what it feels like to be completely at peace, he thought of himself as a little child, resting at his mother's side (Psalm 131:2). When Isaiah spoke of Israel being restored from exile to their former glory, he equated the sense of pure joy and satisfaction to being like a child at his mother's breast and then "carried on her hip and bounced on her lap" (Isaiah 66:12 HCSB).

These ideas are captured in the word *cherish*, which doesn't just mean to love in a general way, but more specifically: "to make warm." It describes a cold, hungry, frightened newborn being placed in the caring arms of his mother. She holds him close and completely wraps her helpless child in the radiating warmth of her embrace and tender love. She nurses and nourishes him. She gently strokes his soft face and tiny hands. She kisses the crown of her baby's head, caressing his soft, delicate hair. She whispers and sings gently into his ears. She comforts and calms his fears. He feels safe and loved. All is well in the warmth of her arms.

That's *cherishing*.

Love gives each of us the opportunity to cherish our children as they grow. Moms may have the more natural temperament and the longest history as the nurturing parent, but men are called to cherish as well. Husbands are commanded to "cherish" and nourish their wives with tender love (Ephesians 5:25–29). When the apostle Paul tried putting into words his love for the churches that he had helped to birth and serve, he said he felt like a "nursing mother" who "tenderly cares for her own children" (1 Thessalonians 2:7). Fathers should warm the hearts of their children in their own way by lavishing them with huge, regular doses of comfort and care through physical, heartwarming affection.

Thankfully, life provides moms and dads with all kinds of everyday chances for this, for all ages of children. Your tender care and loving, appropriate touches race through their nerve endings and carry warmth right into their hearts.

It can be as simple as wrapping your arm around your son's shoulder or taking your daughter's hand. It could be holding them while you watch a movie together or giving a wink and a gentle squeeze on their arm during church. It's sitting at a traffic light and reaching back to pat their knee in the back seat, or stopping them in the hallway for a quick embrace and a kiss on the forehead. Sometimes it's tickling or wrestling with them on the rug in your family room or in a pile of leaves in the backyard.

But even as you're reading this, you may already feel yourself pushing back. You may not be the touchy-feely type. You do better communicating your love through nods, silent smiles, and by providing meat on the table. And that's understandable. Not everyone recalls fond memories of how physical touch was previously extended to them.

But regardless, the loving strength of your touch remains one of the daily, distinct gifts God has given you to capture and cherish the heart of your children. And while you shouldn't feel pressured out of your natural temperament, remember that Jesus appropriately touched children as a blessing to them (Mark 10:16), and your child may truly be missing and longing for the needed warmth your touch could provide. This may even be one of the ways God brings healing to help you redeem a harmful offense from your past and transforms your interaction into healthy, nurturing blessing for your children.

Life can be cold and unpredictable for our kids in a darkening world. Everyday stress can wear on them and beat them down. Sometimes fear and uncertainty can show up like winter, dropping emotional coldness and icy insecurity into their hearts.

But maybe all it takes to begin the thaw is some warm, tender affection from you, as one called by God to be their mother or their father. Your gentle caress on their back or the comfort of your strong embrace could give them emotional strength that calms their worries and self-doubts. And it will likely interweave your hearts ever tighter.

The Bible tells of a man with leprosy who approached Jesus on his knees one day, begging to be healed of his horrible skin disease. Jesus could have answered the sick man's prayer simply by speaking the words and pronouncing him well. Instead, against all cultural custom and personal hygiene, He "reached out his hand and touched him" (Mark 1:41). The healing began with a touch.

Your children need to be cherished. And nothing says it more warmly than your tender touch.

HOW COULD YOU WARM THE LIFE AND
HEART OF YOUR CHILDREN TODAY? TAKE
ADVANTAGE OF A CURRENT OPPORTUNITY
TO GIVE THEM AN UNEXPECTED, TENDER
TOUCH. CHOOSE AN APPROPRIATE
GESTURE THAT SAYS, "I CHERISH YOU,"
AND DO IT WITH SINCERITY.

___ Check here when you've completed today's dare.

What was their response to your affection? Is this something
you need to do more often?

_____

_____

_____

_____

_____

_____

_____

No one ever hated his own flesh, but nourishes and cherishes it. (Ephesians 5:29)

DAY 10
Love is not rude

Give preference to one another in honor. (Romans 12:10)

Little children are wonderfully notorious for their manners.
You cannot help but crack a smile when a newborn belches, a
baby in a restaurant gets spaghetti all over her face, or a toddler
walks into the Christmas party half-dressed and asking mom
for emergency assistance in the bathroom. Their ignorance
supplies free entertainment to an understanding, sympathetic
world.

But as the clock ticks and children become older, the fewer
excuses they and their parents have for poor manners. What
was once tolerated and amusing becomes unacceptable and
irritating.

Perhaps you have endured a child screaming in the theater,
an obnoxious stinker who refuses to take a bath at summer
camp, or a foul-mouthed teenager arguing with his parents in
a department store. In such cases, rudeness can be painfully
unpleasant and awkward for everyone else around. You feel the
ice in the room.

Good manners, on the other hand, create the opposite
effect. They warm the heart and set the atmosphere at ease.
Polite children make your experience with them a fragrance
instead of a stench. They subtly raise the respect level and
enjoyment in the house. Isn't that the kind of effect you want
your children to have on others? To have on you?

By intentionally teaching and modeling good manners
for your children, you not only treat *them* with greater honor
and respect, but you also help them become a living blessing
to others. Parents who do not enjoy being around their own

children need to seriously ask themselves if they have really taken the time to train them how to be considerate, gracious, and likable.

Manners, at their very heart, are a way of expressing love and showing respect for the intrinsic value in other people, each made in the image of God (Genesis 1:27). Respectful etiquette displays a practical, living example of the Golden Rule in action (Luke 6:31). It minimizes unpleasantness by looking out not only "for your own personal interests, but also for the interests of others" (Philippians 2:4). It's how we follow the biblical command to "honor all people" (1 Peter 2:17).

Good manners will not only help you and your children be a walking blessing to others, but will often earn for them special "favor and goodwill" that sets them apart from their peers. That's what the Bible says of Daniel, one of the youths in the Old Testament who "had ability for serving in the king's court" (Daniel 1:4) and found favor with his authorities to the point of being granted special requests (Daniel 1:8–14).

Jesus, too, as a twelve-year-old, was already learning to show respect to his elders, to carry on engaging conversations with them, and to listen attentively as they spoke (Luke 2:46). And He "kept increasing in wisdom and stature, and in favor with God and men" (Luke 2:52). Manners are an important factor in sending blessing out and receiving blessing in return.

Public success in this area begins with what you model privately at home. Let your love for your children alter your own behavior around them. For you, this can be as basic as holding the door for your daughter or thanking your son for doing a good job. Apologizing when you make a mistake. Engaging your children in stimulating conversation and introducing them courteously to your friends or people you meet. Being on time. Eating with proper etiquette. The older children become, the more they default to the manners they have caught from their parents' example. So we all can probably use a refresher course.

Our children need to see us showing ongoing, everyday respect for them, for their mother or father, for neighbors and guests, and for others we interact with.

Manners *grow* on children. They will watch your private etiquette today, make it their public etiquette tomorrow, and then pass it on to their children one day.

We must grow toward a place where rudeness is not tolerated, in either our children or ourselves. A place where no one is made fun of or humiliated, and none of our vocabularies descend to being vulgar, gross, or crude. A place where rolling eyes, biting sarcasm, and pouting are not allowed to become normal patterns of behavior.

Instead, talk about the importance of little things like letting others go first, speaking without mumbling, walking with good posture, and dressing appropriately for each situation. Such habits will not only serve you well for this present season, but serve your children well for a lifetime. Quality manners are a very wise investment toward their future success in friendship, marriage, and in the world.

If you have not done so already, begin instilling in your children the marks of selfless, courteous behavior. Because when you show them which fork to use or how to greet a stranger with a smile, you're not only pinning good form onto their conduct. You are modeling love and giving the deepest parts of their character a daily opportunity to show others the respect they deserve. That's how they learn to bless the world with their presence, and win for themselves a sterling reputation for years to come.

HAVE A MANNERS NIGHT. OPENLY DISCUSS
A FEW WAYS YOU CAN AVOID UNPLEASANT
BEHAVIOR AROUND ONE ANOTHER AND SHOW
GREATER RESPECT. LEAD YOUR FAMILY IN
A FUN MEAL TO PRACTICE GOOD MANNERS,
GIVING EVERYONE A CHANCE TO SERVE AND
BE SERVED. LOCATE A SIMPLE BOOK ON
ETIQUETTE AND BEGIN LEARNING
NEW TIPS AS A FAMILY.

___ Check here when you've completed today's dare.

In what areas do you and your children need to adjust your
manners? What did you learn together as you did this exercise?

_____

_____

_____

_____

_____

_____

_____

He who loves purity of heart and whose speech is gracious,
the king is his friend. (Proverbs 22:11)

DAY 11
Love teaches

These words, which I am commanding you today, shall be on your heart.
You shall teach them diligently to your sons. (Deuteronomy 6:6–7)

How many things do you wish you'd learned before you were an adult, things you've had to figure out on the fly: How to balance a checkbook? How to maintain your car? How to study your Bible? How to have good friendships?

What kind of embarrassing fiascoes could you have avoided if you had known better how to handle yourself in a job interview, how to cook a tender turkey for Thanksgiving, or how to keep from drowning in credit card debt?

Effectively navigating through life means knowing how to solve problems—how to size up a difficult situation, wisely resolve it, and turn things around for good. But without guided preparation and a baseline of skills, you're consistently starting from scratch. Flying blind. Making things up as you go along.

That's where a loving dad and mom come in. Love sees parenting as a workshop. A classroom for success. A boot camp for life's battles. A place where children are continually being trained for life, one little side-by-side adventure at a time. It's everything from tying shoes and riding a bike to parallel parking and ironing a dress shirt.

Love says, "Come here, let me show you something."

"Watch what happens when you do this."

"Don't make the foolish mistake of . . ."

Yes, you could easily solve your daily problems by yourself. It's usually quicker that way. But by inviting a younger audience, and taking a little time to show them how—even to put a task temporarily into their hands—you can build both your relationship and their skill set at the same time.

You can teach your children almost any skill you know how to do if you will just let them *watch* you, then let them *help* you, and then let them *try it* under your supervision.

But it's more than just developing do-it-yourself dexterity and home economics. Love means building up their minds and their relational IQs as well. Melding moral fiber into their core. Developing their worldview with wisdom.

Do your children know what you admire the most about people you respect? Or what you've learned from your greatest mistakes? Try following up a movie night by asking questions about the lead roles and the messages subtly portrayed on-screen. Help your kids discern what belief systems were promoted, what the characters did right and wrong, and what behaviors should be mirrored or avoided in real life.

Ask them, "What's better in the long run . . ." or "What would you do if . . ." to launch lively dinnertime discussions that get everybody thinking.

But there's more. By making your home a learning lab, you also demystify their spiritual training. You make it a natural part of everyday life. When you're able to weave God-honoring concepts into everything from showing hospitality to guests, to sharing vegetables from your garden with neighbors, you communicate that life with God is not a separate category that only happens for a few hours at church. Honoring Him is a daily journey. It can happen on Tuesday at midnight while working on a second-grade art project. Or during pick-up football games in the front yard.

Love simply has a teacher's heart. It knows that "wisdom is better than jewels; and all desirable things cannot compare with her" (Proverbs 8:11). Love is able to serve the carrots and healthy greens of life in a way your kids will receive. And that means long-term nourishment years down the road.

This is what Jesus did with His disciples. He leveraged the moment, saying things like, "Look at the birds of the air . . . your heavenly Father feeds them. . . . Are you not worth much more than they? . . . Do not worry then" (Matthew 6:26–31).

That's why the Bible says to instruct your kids "when you sit in your house and when you walk by the way and when you lie down and when you rise up" (Deuteronomy 6:7). It's deliberate, but also opportunistic. Teachable moments are always waiting around the next corner.

Do you want your children to be set up for success? To minimize their debt and manage their time? To develop a work ethic that gets things done and doesn't quit once the job's no longer fun? To succeed in marriage and family? Do you want them to know the things you already know, to avoid the mistakes you've already made, as well as things you can learn together as you remain curious and teachable yourself? Then you must start being intentional now, redeeming the opportunities you have before you.

Don't save all the deep talks for after they're in bed or after they have graduated from college. Don't plan all your budgets or calendars without showing them how you're doing it. Don't tithe without sharing how they too can honor God with their income (Proverbs 3:9–10). Something that might take you twice as long to do today could save them from twice the problems tomorrow.

Life has enough traps and valleys as it is. But by letting your love draw out the road maps and point out the bridges today, you prepare your children to thank God for you later when they stand and celebrate on the mountain peaks you taught them how to climb. What could love find to teach today?

MAKE TWO SEPARATE LISTS OF THINGS YOU
WANT TO TEACH YOUR KIDS: 1) LIFE SKILLS
AND 2) LIFE LESSONS. KEEP THEM IN A NOTE-
BOOK NEARBY. LOOK FOR AN OPPORTUNITY
TO INVOLVE ONE OR MORE OF YOUR CHILDREN
IN A WORK PROJECT OR SOME OTHER TEACH-
ING MOMENT. MAKE IT A HABIT.

___ Check here when you've completed today's dare.

What did you choose to do with your children? What did they
learn? What did *you* learn?

_____

_____

_____

_____

_____

_____

_____

_____

_____

_____

_____

_____

Let my teaching drop as the rain, my speech distill as the dew. (Deuteronomy 32:2)

Day 12
Love encourages

*Pleasant words are a honeycomb, sweet to the soul
and healing to the bones. (Proverbs 16:24)*

Parents love to hear other people compliment their children. But you may not realize how much your children long to
hear you compliment them directly.

Words are so powerful. The Scripture says, "Death and life
are in the power of the tongue, and those who love it will eat
its fruit" (Proverbs 18:21). What you speak into the ears of your
children can impart love and build bridges of hope for them or
it can poison their perceptions and crush their confidence.

Obviously you don't feel affirming all the time. You may be
dealing with issues in your children that are frankly upsetting,
not flattering. But despite their failures, do your kids still know
that you're their biggest fan? When was the last time they
walked away from a conversation with you with a renewed
sense of acceptance, courage, and confidence?

The fruit of your lips not only helps them define their reality and comprehend their identity but also guides their destiny.
Too often parents unknowingly curse their children by ridicul-
ing them, calling them names, or telling them what a failure
they will likely be in the future. Ten seconds of verbal venom
could completely taint their lives forever. So it is vital that we
bridle our tongues (James 1:26; 3:2–12).

We should always guard the descriptions we attach to our
children. There is a big difference between telling your son he
did something foolish and actually calling him a fool.

God repeatedly changed people's names to honor them,
encourage them, and help them view themselves differently

(Genesis 17:5; 32:28; John 1:42). Our children need to humbly realize that they are sinners, but still see themselves as beloved by God, made in His image, and blessed by you, their parents.

We must allow the patience and kindness of love to guide our tongues and build an atmosphere of powerful encouragement. Our mouths should be nourishing wells of love and truth, not polluted springs of cursing, complaining, and insults.

Paul said it this way: "Do not let any unwholesome talk come out of your mouths, but only what is helpful for building others up according to their needs, that it may benefit those who listen" (Ephesians 4:29 NIV). Finding fault should never be our default. Kids who are constantly worried about being scolded after every error will wither under the weight of your words. Though God could exhibit many embarrassing things against any of us, the Bible reveals Him as one who delights over His children "with shouts of joy" (Zephaniah 3:17).

How often do your kids hear you bragging on them in public? How often do you stop to reemphasize your love or highlight something you admire? Think what it does for their budding aspirations when they know they can count on your encouragement to try a new challenge. When they're confident you'll be there to support them, win or lose, they're freed up to take their very best swing at even a difficult task.

Take your encouragement to the next level by making your kind words to them delightful, deliberate, and daily.

Delightful. It's uplifting when they discover something you personally enjoy about them. Mention to your spouse what you really like about your children, loud enough for them to hear in the other room. Your praise will leap inside their hearts and may echo back and forth in their ears for years to come.

You can begin an unforgettable conversation by asking, "Do you know what I really like about you?" Or respond to an accomplishment with, "Wow! I'm impressed! You're really good at that." Even if they haven't done anything praiseworthy at the moment, it is always good to spontaneously wrap your arms around them and whisper, "I'm so glad that God put you in our family." These words will be gold to them.

Deliberate. Be strategic with your words. Whatever you choose to compliment will be what your children will value more and seek to duplicate in the future. So be careful to affirm inner character more than merely outward appearance or public performance. Pointing out how proud you are of their honesty, diligence, and kindness strengthens their moral foundations more in the long run than telling them you like their hairstyle or the socks they're wearing today. Aim your words at the heart, where it counts the most.

Recognize that your encouragement can also steer the paths they decide to take later on. Aim wisely. Saying, "Great job on that painting! I love your attention to detail," may fuel their desire to continue developing skill in that area.

Daily. Because any child could potentially be discouraged or off-track at any time, we should verbally challenge and inspire them as an ongoing habit. "Encourage one another day after day, as long as it is still called 'Today,' so that none of you will be hardened by the deceitfulness of sin" (Hebrews 3:13).

Love stays busy looking for reasons to affirm good character and behavior in our kids, no matter how old they get. Even if your children are grown, you can still find ways to highlight the little things they do that make you proud.

The more you celebrate in their lives now, the higher you lift their wings, giving you even greater reasons to celebrate in the future. So open your mouth and let your love fly!

TODAY'S DARE

COMMIT TO MENTIONING POSITIVE
ATTRIBUTES ABOUT YOUR KIDS EVERY DAY
THROUGHOUT THE COMING WEEK. DO IT
BOTH PRIVATELY TO THEM AS WELL AS
PUBLICLY TO FRIENDS AND FAMILY.

___ Check here when you've completed today's dare.

What attributes came to mind for each of your children? How
did you express it to them? What was their response?

_____

_____

_____

_____

_____

_____

_____

_____

_____

_____

_____

Encourage one another and build up one another,
just as you also are doing. (1 Thessalonians 5:11)

DAY 13
Love disciplines

Know in your heart that the LORD your God was disciplining you just as a man disciplines his son. (Deuteronomy 8:5)

When our children misbehave, we do them no favors by ignoring or glossing over it. Love compels us to wisely discipline. This is one way God expresses love to His children. "My son, do not reject the discipline of the LORD . . . for whom the LORD loves He reproves, even as a father corrects the son in whom he delights" (Proverbs 3:11–12).

The more you love your children, the less foolishness and rebellion you will tolerate or ignore. "He who spares his rod hates his son, but he who loves him disciplines him promptly" (Proverbs 13:24 NKJV). For though discipline is unwanted and unpleasant, it ultimately trains a child's mind to think wisely and his heart to submit respectfully (Proverbs 22:15).

"No discipline seems enjoyable at the time, but painful. Later on, however, it yields the fruit of peace and righteousness to those who have been trained by it" (Hebrews 12:11 HCSB).

We must help our kids discover that their actions come with real consequences, and that greater freedom, a peaceful conscience, and lasting joys come from practicing good behavior and godly character. Scripture says our heavenly Father "disciplines us for our good," so that we can mature and be more like Him (Hebrews 12:10).

So we need to evaluate honestly the condition of our own hearts whenever we refuse to correct our children. And to ask if we are more interested in keeping the peace for the moment than strengthening their character for the rest of their lives.

As easy as it is to keep excusing misbehavior—whether from our own fatigue or from fear of a child's anger and resistance—love steps in to courageously say and do what is needed. That's what God's love does for us as His children.

Consider the levels of His discipline. He exhorts and instructs us clearly while sharing with us the consequences of disobedience beforehand. If we resist, He warns or rebukes us. Then He will also lovingly "chasten" and "scourge" us with painful and appropriate consequences when we rebel (Hebrews 12:5–6). He is patient, but never a pushover.

Likewise, parents, especially fathers, are instructed to train up their children in the nurture and admonition of the Lord (Ephesians 6:4). *Nurture* includes teaching clear instructions and chastening when rules are broken. But *admonition* goes deeper by appealing to their consciences with the knowledge that God is ultimately the One they are to honor and obey.

If our children don't develop a fundamental respect for God, they will have no lasting foundation for true moral decision making in the future. His character and commands are the *why* behind *what* we teach them. Lying is wrong because God is truth and has commanded us to walk in truth. Bitterness and hatred are in opposition to His love and commands. All authorities represent His authority. If we don't train our kids to obey us "as unto the Lord," we are merely training them to further disobey God in the future.

The Bible gives the example of Eli, the revered Hebrew priest whose two sons had become infamous for their cheating, stealing, and immorality. They frustrated their father, but he avoided confronting their indiscretions. This upset God, who then asked of Eli, "Why do you . . . honor your sons above Me?" (1 Samuel 2:29; 3:13). Instead of rebuking them, Eli had placed his blind love for their present happiness ahead of God's call to train them before the Lord. What felt like love for his children had ironically become a destructive disregard of their souls. Like Eli, when we refuse to discipline, our long-term love is ultimately in question.

If you don't train your children to respect and take you seriously in today's battle, you will lose a thousand other battles down the road. Love does not run from problems; it willingly pays the parental price. When children sin, love steps in. To explain what's wrong and why. To enforce what's best for them. To boldly confront foolishness and rebellion. To establish clear consequences and boundaries.

The Bible does not advocate hateful or harmful abuse, but it does call for appropriate discipline that is *painful enough* to get the job done and cause your children to respect your authority, so they'll never want to repeat the misbehavior again. Children do not take seriously parents who lecture, nag, and threaten but never follow through with any punishment worth fearing. Actions and consequences give weight to your words.

If you said your child would be spanked or grounded or lose a privilege if they did something wrong, then you must keep your promise. Otherwise, your words become empty and you are seen as full of hot air, or worse, a liar.

Yes, discipline must be balanced out with patience, grace, and mercy. You should always guard your children's hearts and explain your decisions lovingly, clearly, and fairly, knowing that kids can sour if you're operating out of uncontrolled anger or if the consequence is out of balance with the crime. But our world doesn't need any more dishonorable kids who get away with as much as they can. Love drives us to raise children of honor and responsibility. Who love God and walk in integrity. Who are a blessing to their families and to society. And this requires a parent's love that dares to discipline.

PRAY THROUGH THE METHODS YOU USE FOR
DISCIPLINE. ARE THEY EFFECTIVE?
DO THEY CONTAIN BOTH THE CORRECTION
OF BEHAVIOR AS WELL AS AN APPEAL TO THE
CONSCIENCE? PURPOSE TO USE DIRECT BUT
FAIR DISCIPLINE IN THE FUTURE, AND MAKE
EFFORTS TO BALANCE YOUR ACTIONS WITH
THE GOAL OF HONORING THE LORD.

___ Check here when you've completed today's dare.

What changes, if any, could you make to ensure that you are
disciplining your children with both nurture and admonition?

_For further reading, see "What Does the Bible Say about Spanking?"
on page 202 in the appendix._

The commandment is a lamp and the teaching is light;
and reproofs for discipline are the way of life. (Proverbs 6:23)

DAY 14

Love is compassionate

Just as a father has compassion on his children,
so the Lord has compassion on those who fear Him. (Psalm 103:13)

If it hasn't happened already, days are likely coming when your children will be forced to face the inevitable dark clouds of life. Heartbreaking disappointments. Devastating failures. Unexpected bad news. Confusion, anxiety, and stress.

These may blow in as the loss of their prized possession, a failure at school, the cruelty of another child's words, or even the shame of their own sin or misconduct. In any case, these moments afford parents the ideal opportunity to display one of the most cherished characteristics in life . . . *compassion.*

It's what we all long for from others when we are hurting, burdened, or ashamed. It's what we admire in those who give to the poor or serve the disabled and downtrodden.

Compassion is simply choosing to feel sincerely concerned and sympathetic because of the heavy burden another person is under, then being willing to do something about it. It means listening to someone's struggles instead of discounting their discomfort. Taking the time to wipe away a tear instead of allowing another to be shed. Covering shame instead of exposing it. Sharing the load instead of ignoring it.

When people are hurting, they thirst for drops of mercy from any source and will run toward anyone who will share some compassion. As a parent, your compassion lovingly shouts, "I care!" when your children are convinced that nobody does. And that's why it's such a vitally important, God-given trait to exhibit.

Difficult situations in our children's lives are incredible opportunities for us to prove that we're a safe refuge to run to with their burdens and brokenness. If we pass over their pain without offering an ear or any help, then our kids will not likely feel welcome later on when matters get more serious.

In contrast, the *compassionless* are always viewed as selfish and heartless. Cold and callous. Sensing a *lack* of compassion is why workers go on strike, teenagers rebel, wives walk out on husbands, and citizens overthrow their dictators.

Compassion is not always easy or automatic. It is rarely convenient or comfortable. But your love should refuse to leave any doubt in your children that you take their burdens seriously. They should see you as an oasis of care and concern, not a dry desert that offers no relief. But for this to happen, you must lead your heart to be available and understanding. As impressionable as children are, what if your son or daughter learned that your voice was the first one they could quickly turn to when they needed comfort or counsel?

Jesus, as always, serves as the model of love's greatest attributes, including the merciful warmth of compassion. Amazingly, He set examples of how to show it to . . .

- the *weary*, the "distressed and dispirited" (Matthew 9:36)
- the *ignorant*, like "sheep without a shepherd" (Mark 6:34)
- the *disorganized* who were overwhelmed (Mark 8:1–3)
- the greatly *indebted* (Matthew 18:27)
- the *mourning* who had lost a loved one (Luke 7:12–14)
- the broken *sinner* (Luke 15:20–21)
- the *abused and needy* (Luke 10:31–35)

Jesus allowed Himself to be "moved with compassion" and personally feel the sorrows and burdens others were feeling. Then He went into action to lighten their load. In fact, within these seven "compassions" of Jesus, you'll find a fairly complete picture of His salvation: how He came to us when we were *wearied* by sin, spiritually *indebted* to Him, *ignorant* of how to clear ourselves, *unprepared* to face God and eternity. Though He is *saddened* and painfully aware of our *wickedness*, He offers the *needed* forgiveness that His loving sacrifice can provide (Romans 5:8).

He said, "Come to Me, all who are weary and heavy-laden, and I will give you rest. Take My yoke upon you and learn from Me, for I am gentle and humble in heart, and you will find rest for your souls. For My yoke is easy and My burden is light" (Matthew 11:28–30). He can meet us in our crisis when our hearts cry out to Him. He is faithful to sympathize with our weaknesses (Hebrews 4:15–16) and respond to our prayers.

Likewise, your willingness to comfort and console your children will draw them close and keep them coming. Instead of having to struggle alone with spiritual doubts and questions, hoping you never find out what they've done, staying worried by changes in their body, or feeling insecure because of what their peers are saying, they'll know that your door and heart are always open for their confessions and concerns.

Yes, there are key moments when you should tell them to quit throwing a pity party and start growing up. Or to realize that life is not fair and people can be cruel. Or that they need to repent of their own sins and get right with God. But this type of coaching and discipline needs to be balanced with enough tender moments of compassion that they know you deeply care about them, that your love is willing to feel their grief and bear their burdens (Galatians 6:1–2).

It's being the tender hands of Jesus. It's wrapping your arms around them instead of wringing their necks. It's knowing when to step in and rescue instead of leaving them in a ditch. It's the beautiful healing of consolation.

TODAY'S DARE

LOOK AND LISTEN FOR OPPORTUNITIES TO
DEMONSTRATE COMPASSION TO YOUR
CHILDREN AND HELP LIGHTEN THEIR LOAD
IN AREAS WHERE IT MAY BE TOO HEAVY.
ASK IF YOU COULD PRAY FOR THEM ABOUT
AN ISSUE THEY'VE RECENTLY SHARED.

___ Check here when you've completed today's dare.

What opportunities did you find to show compassion? What
was the result?

_____

_____

_____

_____

_____

_____

_____

_____

_____

_____

_____

May Your compassion come to me that I may live. (Psalm 119:77)

DAY 15
Love is from God

Let us love one another,
because love is from God. (1 John 4:7 HCSB)

The love that parents have for their children is one of the strongest of all human emotions. From holding your newborn in your arms, cheering for your son as he rounds the bases, or walking your daughter down the aisle, the parental affection we enjoy is beautiful and powerful.

The Greek word *storge* (pronounced STOR-gay) describes this family love and natural affection we feel for our blood relatives, especially for our children.

You may be familiar with the word *eros*, which is a romantic, physical love between lovers, or *phileo*, which is the brotherly love and fondness we feel for close friends. But *storge*, *eros*, and *phileo* all share some constraints. They are limited by human ability, greatly influenced by feelings, and can change depending upon circumstances. Even selfish, evil people can momentarily stir up and feel these types of love toward their spouse, children, or friends at various times.

A stronger love exists than all of these, however—the truest, purest, and greatest love of all. It is unselfish and puts others first. It is unconditional and sacrifices most. And it is unstoppable because it "bears all things, believes all things, hopes all things, endures all things" (1 Corinthians 13:7).

The Greek word *agape* (uh-GOP-ay) refers to the love that God commands us to demonstrate most throughout our lives. *Agape* is unique because it is not based upon feelings, circumstances, or the behavior of the one being loved. This is the amazing love that God has for us as His children—the love we can have for *our* children—the love we are actually describing each day throughout this book.

Because our parental love is limited by our human capacity and polluted by our sinfulness, the key to loving our children unconditionally with *agape* love is not to try harder, but to tap into its pure and perfect source. "Beloved, let us (*agape*) love one another, for (*agape*) love is from God" (1 John 4:7).

Our parental love is a small puddle compared to the river of God's unconditional love for us. But by connecting to Him and His never-ending supply, the love we can have for our children can actually be *God's* love for them. It can surge through us the way a river carries water from a higher source. His love—His Fatherly love (1 John 3:1)—is what gives us as parents the capability to love more unselfishly and unconditionally.

Stop and think about that, especially if you don't have a history of being loved well by a father, or if you worry your love for your kids isn't enough, no matter how hard you try. The truth is, the love God can give you to shower upon your children is infinitely stronger than your parental love alone. It is fortified by His love, the source and fountain of *all* love.

We need to find rest in this truth. God our Father is much more invested in our kids than we are. So part of our goal as parents is communicating to our kids that God's love for them is where *real* love comes from, along with their ultimate value as individuals. He is the One who loved them and uniquely created them. And His love can sustain them, no matter who rejects or disappoints them in life. "Even if my father and mother abandon me," His Word says, "the LORD cares for me" (Psalm 27:10 HCSB).

So it's not actually their cute expressions or youthful charm that enables us to love our children the way we should. Nor does any lack of respect or self-control mean we love them any less. We love them because "God is love" (1 John 4:16) and because "He first loved us" (1 John 4:19).

When we look at our children—whether they're babies, teenagers, or beyond—we see individuals created "in His own image" (Genesis 1:27). And though they are tainted with human sin (Psalm 51:5), their Father in heaven has still chosen to love them with His perfect, *agape* love (Romans 5:8).

Every day, with each new dare, always bear in mind this one pervasive, reorienting truth: *you are handling a divine opportunity to experience and represent the love of God.* Our children are not playthings to be merely photographed or conveniences to make our lives complete. They're not barriers to our freedom or monuments to our greatness. They may please us and make us proud. They may fail us and disappoint us. But our children are ultimately not about *us.* They are about the One who gave them to us, and about the love He has for them.

He loves your children more than you do. And you will love them more than you do now if you allow His love to flow into you and then into them through you. This happens by faith. This happens by turning to the greatest expression of God's love, His Son (John 15:13). And it happens as we daily walk with Him and pray, "Heavenly Father, I receive your perfect and unconditional love for me and pray that you will love my children through me as well. Make me a channel of your perfect love."

Why do we have children at all? *Because God loves them and has chosen to share them with us.* What does our relationship with them represent? A *living picture of God's love for Jesus and His love for us.* What determines their value in our eyes? *The immense love God has for them.* What are our goals in raising them? *To honor Him and love Him . . . by how we love them.*

Like God loves them. And like He loves us.

TODAY'S DARE

IF POSSIBLE, REMIND YOUR CHILDREN TODAY
THAT "GOD IS LOVE" (1 JOHN 4:16) AND THAT
HE DEEPLY LOVES THEM. PRAY WITH THEM
THAT THEY WILL ALWAYS KNOW THEY CAN
CALL ON HIM AS THEIR LOVING, HEAVENLY
FATHER. AND PRAY FOR YOURSELF, THAT GOD
WILL HELP YOU RECEIVE HIS LOVE FOR YOU
AND MAKE YOU A CHANNEL OF HIS LOVE TO
YOUR CHILDREN (JOHN 15:9).

___ Check here when you've completed today's dare.

What was the result of your interaction? Has God revealed anything new and refreshing to you about His love and the way
you can love your children?

_____

_____

_____

_____

_____

_____

_____

You are my Father, my God, and the rock of my salvation. (Psalm 89:26)

DAY 16
Love respects God

The fear of the LORD *is the beginning of knowledge.* (Proverbs 1:7)

We teach our children to be careful to avoid oncoming traffic, poisonous snakes, and the shocking combination of an electrical outlet with a butter knife. But there is one appropriate fear that will not only protect them but actually bring honor and blessing into their lives.

It is the reverent fear of God.

Did you know that parents are commanded to teach their children to fear God so they can live better and longer lives? (Deuteronomy 6:1–13). A healthy fear of the Lord is the foundational key that enables our children to think more wisely, speak more honorably, and live in a way that's more pleasing to God.

We should echo the invitation of David, who said, "Come, you children, listen to me; I will teach you the fear of the LORD" (Psalm 34:11). The fear of the Lord is a deep respect for the One who is all-powerful and completely holy. It is not a cause to flee from God, but rather a greater reason to run to Him and fall on our knees before Him. He is so pure and powerful that fearing Him teaches us—parents and children alike—to take His rule and commands very, very seriously.

God is not only patient, kind, and loving, but also holy, powerful, and completely just. He will never be mocked, disregarded, or ignored without consequence (Galatians 6:7). He reigns supreme, with heaven and earth under His feet (Matthew 28:18; 1 Corinthians 15:27). The Bible describes Him as a "consuming fire" that we should serve with reverence and awe (Hebrews 12:29). The fear of the Lord awakens wisdom within us as we realize that we are living in a universe completely under His control (Matthew 28:18; Psalm 103:19).

It begins with an awareness of God's *presence*. We cannot run or hide from Him (Psalm 139:1–12). He omnisciently knows our every thought, desire, and motivation. His pure eyes see everything we do (Proverbs 15:3).

Second, this fear makes us conscious of His unlimited *power*. He omnipotently holds our lives and eternal destiny in His hands. Jesus said, "Do not fear those who kill the body but are unable to kill the soul; but rather fear Him who is able to destroy both soul and body in hell" (Matthew 10:28). We must never lose our awe at what His grace has and can save us from. He is not forgetful and grandfatherly. His power over us is only eclipsed by the loving might of His mercy.

Third, the fear of the Lord reminds us to be very respectful of God's *holiness* as One who is set apart, infinitely greater and higher than everything else. Perfect in every way. To approach Him would be like trying to approach the sun. To comprehend Him would be like an ant attempting to swallow the ocean.

When a man and his children learn to fear the Lord, they begin to hate evil, pride, and perversion (Proverbs 8:13) and "avoid the snares of death" (Proverbs 14:27). This fear can help a little girl to stop lying and a teenage boy to quit acting immorally, as they discover a holy God sees them.

One of the Bible's great warnings is against those who belittle or ignore God. Some people foolishly think He can be disregarded or outsmarted, though "He counts the number of the stars" and "His understanding is infinite" (Psalm 147:4–5). If the people of the world feared God, they would stop stealing and killing, hating and hurting, and begin walking in humble respect for Him and one another.

One of the overlooked ways we as parents should bless our children is by honoring the Lord with our own personal, humble worship. Not just church-service attendance, but an authentic love that flows with obedience and reverence for God in every place. We should respect Him so much that we refuse to live in any way that is displeasing to Him.

"How blessed is the man who fears the LORD," the Bible says, "who greatly delights in His commandments. His descendants will be mighty on earth; the generation of the upright will be blessed" (Psalm 112:1–2). David wrote, "How great is Your goodness, which You have stored up for those who fear You" (Psalm 31:19).

The fear of the Lord is a "fountain of life" that can cause all our other fears to go away (Proverbs 14:26–27). It not only keeps us from sinful actions, but it opens the floodgates for blessings. Wisdom, counsel, and understanding. Wealth, honor, and fruitfulness. God's presence and provision.

So the fear of God may be one of the most important things you could ever pray for and seek to develop in the hearts of your children. As they learn to respect Him, they will respect life and respect you. The more you talk with them about the greatness of God and their need to reverence and honor Him, you can help them see the lovingkindness embedded in His power, that's more than able to guide and care for them.

For He is awe-inspiring, but He is also intimate. He is almighty and yet all-merciful. Serving a God this big is not a burden but a sacred privilege. The more your children fear Him, the more they can know Him and humbly love Him, enlightening and aligning their hearts with His greatness.

To deny Him is only the beginning of tears and years of regret. But to fear God is the starting point of the best and most abundant life of all.

ASK YOUR CHILDREN TO READ PSALM 139
WITH YOU. THEN ASK WHAT THEY LEARNED
ABOUT WHERE GOD IS AND WHAT HE KNOWS
ABOUT EACH OF US. EXPLAIN HOW GOD
CREATED THEM, LOVES THEM, ALWAYS SEES
THEM, AND WILL JUDGE THEM ONE DAY FOR
HOW THEY LIVED THEIR LIVES. FINISH BY
PRAYING VERSES 23–24 TOGETHER.

___ Check here when you've completed today's dare.

How did your children receive this truth? What did they say
about these verses you read? How can this Scripture make a
difference in the way they think and the way you parent?

_____

_____

_____

_____

_____

_____

_____

He will bless those who fear the LORD, the small together with the great. (Psalm 115:13)

DAY 17
Love seeks God's blessing

*You make him most blessed forever; You make him joyful
with gladness in Your presence. (Psalm 21:6)*

Parents hope their children show up healthy and grow up
happy. Safe and secure. Loved and blessed. But what does that
really mean? What does *blessed* look like in a child, teenager,
or young adult? The word actually carries with it the idea of
being favored, fruitful, and fulfilled. Successful and satisfied.
Possessing reasons to rejoice and be glad.

Yes, we all want our kids to be blessed. Strong. Wise.
Skillful. Joyful. Blessed with great friendships and healthy marriages. But who is the person God blesses? And how can our
children experience it?

First, did you know your personal faith and relationship
with God can invite Him to greatly bless your children? The
Scripture says, "How blessed is everyone who fears the LORD,
who walks in His ways," for this causes your children to grow
"like olive plants around your table," fruitful, strong, and pros-
pering (Psalm 128:1, 3). God said He blessed Abraham's descendants because of Abraham's great faith (Genesis 17:6–8). He
later said to His people on the borders of the Promised Land, "I
have set before you life and death, the blessing and the curse.
So choose life in order that you may live, you and your descendants, by loving the LORD your God, by obeying His voice, and
by holding fast to Him" (Deuteronomy 30:19–20).

So if you walk in faith and integrity—loving, fearing, and
obeying God—His Word reveals that He will bless you for it,
and your children as well.

In addition to this, Jesus described several loving, selfless attitudes we should develop that will cause us to be blessed and blissfully fulfilled regardless of our surroundings or circumstances (Matthew 5:3–12). And while these "beatitudes" don't come naturally, we do give our children a much better chance of growing into them the earlier we start teaching, modeling, and championing them at home. Jesus said...

"Blessed are the poor in spirit." Being "poor in spirit" is a moment-by-moment dependence upon God's strength, Spirit, and wisdom rather than our own. It recognizes that forgiveness and salvation are supplied by Him, not conjured from within. It makes prayer more perpetual, knowing that being loving and doing good each day happens only with God's help, not because we have all the answers or the power. Young kids feel indestructible, but they still need God's guidance and protection every day. As parents, we should make our homes prayerful places where we lead one another to humbly admit our need and ask for God's powerful, enabling grace.

"Blessed are those who mourn." God promises to comfort and bless those who mourn about the things that make Him mourn. A child's life should include much fun and laughter but still recognize that many things are not funny. Like violence and abuse, a close friend's pain, or the loss of a loved one. Love does not laugh at sin; it is broken by it (Ezekiel 9:4). It grieves the plight of the poor, national tragedy, death, and hell. Seeing that life can be ugly and painful, children learn that truly caring for God and others means sometimes shedding some tears. Love balances joyful expression with tearful discretion.

"Blessed are the gentle." Love is not restless and resistant, putting down others or acting superior. It humbles us and sees everyone else as equal or more important. For younger kids, this means sharing, taking turns, and not spoiling the party by

being so bossy. For older kids, it may mean cheering and being a team player instead of sulking because you're not getting the ball or the glory enough. The traditional Bible word here is *meek*—which does not mean *weak*, but rather keeping your "strength under control." It means not having to outmuscle, outshine, or overshadow others. You keep your head from swelling and others from feeling small.

"*Blessed are those who hunger and thirst for righteousness.*" We should long to live right and to stay right with God and others—to "hunger" for that. Most kids know what it's like to crave their favorite foods. But maybe you could find a teachable moment to help them see that intimately knowing God and hungering to live God's way will satisfy them better than anything this world can offer (Psalm 16:11; 37:4; 63:5).

"*Blessed are the merciful*"—those who forgive others, live with compassion for the needy, and walk with a servant's heart ready to help. "*Blessed are the pure in heart*"—those who aren't two different people when in two different settings but walk in integrity and willingly repent when they fail. "*Blessed are the peacemakers*"—those who rush in to quell disagreements and help people find peace with one another and also with God.

Finally, "*blessed are those who have been persecuted,*" Jesus said, when it's a backlash against their good character, their Christian faith, or their unapologetic stand for principle. Our kids should learn to rejoice if they have God's approval, whether the world agrees or not. In the long run, we know where compromise will take our kids —and it's not toward a lifetime enjoying the richest of God's blessings.

Love wants our children to be healthy, happy, and thriving in whatever they do. We dream of it and work for it. That's why love chooses a proven path to take them there: God's "blessed" promises for children of all ages. Start it in your home.

ASK YOURSELF IF YOUR LIFESTYLE IS
INVITING GOD'S BLESSING ON YOUR FAMILY
OR REPELLING IT. WHAT NEEDS TO CHANGE?
SECOND, CHOOSE TWO OR MORE OF THE
ATTRIBUTES MENTIONED TODAY AND DISCUSS
THEM WITH YOUR CHILDREN AT A MEAL.
THEN PRAY FOR GOD TO INSTILL A THIRST
WITHIN BOTH THEM AND YOURSELF TO
DEVELOP THESE ATTITUDES IN YOUR LIVES.

___ Check here when you've completed today's dare.

What things about your family came to mind as you read this
day? Which attributes did you choose and why? What did you
pick up from your conversation?

_____

_____

_____

_____

_____

_____

_____

It is the blessing of the LORD that makes rich, and He adds no sorrow to it. (Proverbs 10:22)

DAY 18
Love models the way

Marriage is to be held in honor among all. (Hebrews 13:4)

The Bible contains many examples of people who sought help from God and then received a wise, though unexpected answer. Naaman, an army chief, was angry after being told by the prophet Elisha to go wash himself in the Jordan River if he wanted a cure for his leprosy (2 Kings 5:10–12). A materialistic, young ruler walked away frustrated after Jesus said to "sell all that you possess and distribute it to the poor . . . and come, follow Me" (Luke 18:22).

God knows we will not always understand or like His solutions to our situations. So when you come to Him with a desire to love your children more fully, don't be surprised if one of His most important requests seems unexpected: *to love and respect your spouse more fully as well.*

Children stand and grow on the foundation of their parents' relationship. The more you show genuine love and respect for your mate or your ex, the stronger and more loved your children will feel. Love is not merely heard and taught; it is seen and caught.

Marriage is one of God's primary ways of teaching us how to love another selfish sinner unconditionally. This is the best environment in which children should ideally grow. But any romance can turn sour if love is not leading the way. Bickering and bitterness can become as common as the nightly setting sun. And what do our kids feel and learn when this happens? Insecurity, anxiety, and anger. How do they interpret and grasp the meaning of love when their parents are constantly fighting? They struggle to receive it within this sea of relational dysfunction.

Your interaction with your child's other parent may be amazing, mediocre, or a minefield, but it is still the primary example affecting your children's lives. You may have gone through a painful divorce, and opportunities still present themselves to fuss over the phone or complain to the children about their absent father or irritable mother. But what kind of confusion does this set up in a child's heart—hearing words of love from each parent in their own ears, yet seeing them act unloving and hostile toward each other?

Regardless of your current marital standing, Jesus commands you to love your child's other parent, whether they're your close friend (John 15:13), distant neighbor (Luke 10:25–37), or arch-enemy (Luke 6:27–29). Love is not optional in God's relational economy. Though love does not always equal trust or intimacy in every dynamic, it should still inspire daily, consistent examples of patience and kindness, no matter what the other has done in the past. Being faithful, warm, understanding, and cooperative with your wife or husband may not always be easy, but it will cash out in your children's hearts as security, peace, strength, and greater self-acceptance.

Obviously, you cannot completely control the climate in your house. You yourself may be working hard for unity, yet still be dealt dysfunction in return. But loving your kids means doing your part to cool things down. To swallow your pride. To ask forgiveness for your own faults. To listen. To affirm. To open your eyes and see how much of what is being said by your spouse (or ex) may be more true than you've been willing to admit. Any loving changes you can make will not only look better on *you*; they're very likely to show up as more welcoming smiles and more pleasant mealtimes with your whole family. It may not fix everything, but it could get your ship moving in the right direction.

Fathers, the greater responsibility for leading the way begins with you. How easy it can be to feel disrespected, then take out your frustrated ego on your wife and belittle her in front of your kids. Not only is this dishonorable, foolish, and unloving, but your children will often project your disapproval of their beloved mother onto themselves, receiving it as a cloaked dissatisfaction with them too.

Both parents should model what healthy relationships look like for their children. Speaking negatively and turning a child's heart against the other parent is not love. Your words and attitudes should cause them to respect their other parent more, not less. We should make the "honor thy parents" command something that's easier for our children to do, not harder.

It is OK to respectfully disagree behind closed doors, but a father and mother should always be a united front and in total agreement when they are in front of their children, because you are defining the concepts of marriage, unity, communication, and reconciliation in their growing minds. They will naturally tend to follow your example, whether it is one of love or bitterness. And they will tend to pass your example on to your grandchildren and great-grandchildren.

No matter what your spouse or ex-spouse has done, your forgiveness can disarm much of the damage and keep it from raining down on your children's heads and into their hearts. And regardless of what *you've* done, you can determine to change and model kindness again. Be patient if things take longer to resolve than you think they should. But as best as you can, and with God's help, prayerfully raise your respect and love level for the other parent. You will be doing one of the most loving things your kids could ever hope for.

TODAY'S DARE

ASK GOD TO GIVE YOU A GREATER LOVE AND
RESPECT FOR YOUR SPOUSE (OR YOUR CHILD'S
OTHER PARENT). SHARE SOMETHING ENCOUR-
AGING AND POSITIVE TODAY ABOUT THEM TO
YOUR CHILDREN. IF YOU HAVE BEEN RUNNING
THEM DOWN AROUND YOUR KIDS, ASK YOUR
CHILDREN TO FORGIVE YOU.

___ Check here when you've completed today's dare.

What did you say to your children? How did they respond?

_____

_____

_____

_____

_____

_____

_____

_____

Let love be without hypocrisy. (Romans 12:9)

DAY 19
Love protects

The LORD *will protect you from all evil;*
He will keep your soul. (Psalm 121:7)

Let's face it: the world is getting worse, not better. There
aren't too many neighborhoods anymore where kids can
safely wander around all afternoon till their mothers blink the
porch light for supper. Threats to their physical safety and the
forces at work against their developing beliefs are on the rise.
Television, video games, and the Internet are exposing children
to evil much sooner and more often. And no matter how many
people call you overbearing for insisting on knowing where
everybody is and who they're with, your job is not to please
them. Your job is to parent.

And that means being a protector.

Scripture shows the mother of Moses protecting her young
son from the dangerous threat against his life and safety
(Exodus 2:2). It shows Joseph the carpenter transferring Jesus
twice to new living conditions, protecting the young Messiah
from the murderous intentions of the king (Matthew 2:13–14,
22). It also reveals Solomon warning his son against foolish
friends (Proverbs 13:20), bad business deals (Proverbs 6:1–5),
and loose women (Proverbs 5:1–14).

The psalmist tells us that "the angel of the LORD encamps
around those who fear Him, and rescues them" (Psalm 34:7).
How glad are you that God is attentive to where you are and
that He invites you to take "refuge" in Him? (Psalm 34:8). Why
should your kids not enjoy a similar comfort of knowing that
your love deeply cares about their well-being?

Love "always protects" (1 Corinthians 13:7 NIV). It leads us to protect their minds, bodies, hearts, and purity. Instead of exposing them to situations way over their heads, love wisely keeps moral confusion and shock values to a minimum. Instead of leaving them to their own immaturity and peer persuasion, love trains them to put on their seat belts early, and it establishes moral guardrails to handle life's unexpected turns. It also keeps those boundaries in place until our kids are ready to handle greater liberties and responsibilities.

Love watches out. It has their back. It can say "No!" even in the face of outrage. And it is willing to be the bad guy in order to be a good parent.

That's because you're not only protecting your kids from getting into trouble; you're protecting their long-term freedom and opportunities. The same love that doesn't turn them loose to wander the city on Friday night is also helping to keep their testimony and reputation clean. The same love that keeps the computer in a central room is also offering a life more free from endless distractions or unbridled addictions.

Count on culture to be continually pushing down the age range at which they think your kids are ready to handle depravity. Gruesome violence. Sexual knowledge. Foul language. Full online access.

But remember, your kids don't belong to them. And neither is it your job to please someone who has not been assigned the privilege of passing on a stronger family heritage. The Bible reminds us that we have been commissioned by God to keep watch over our children's souls and that we will give an account to Him one day of how we handled this responsibility (Hebrews 13:17).

Your kids grow up fast enough. But by using your parental clout to block the pressure that's pushing against them, you give yourself more time to win their hearts and mold their maturity. By not being a rubber-stamped permission slip, you can allow them to gradually test new waters with wisdom instead of being led into the dark and right off a cliff.

Protectiveness is not merely restriction. It's not just avoiding the negative and letting nothing come along to fill its place. It's overcoming the tide of evil with a tidal wave of good (Romans 12:21). It's surrounding them with good books, great music, and godly friends. It's helping them learn "the difference between the holy and the profane . . . to discern between the unclean and the clean" (Ezekiel 44:23). It's pressing pause on the remote and talking openly about what was right or wrong about that last movie scene. By helping them learn to discern and by strengthening their resistance skills, you will equip them with the portable protection they'll need whenever they leave your watch.

But for now, you're in charge of your home. You're the coach who determines the drills and prepares them for battle. You must determine the balance of when to press down and surround and when to lighten up and let them learn. In order to gear them up today to win tomorrow, consider these three key attributes you should pray for and develop in your children:

1. A moral discernment of right and wrong (Hebrews 5:14)
2. An appetite for good and a hatred for evil (Romans 12:9)
3. A courageous willingness to stand alone under pressure (Daniel 1:8–16)

Use these strategically, and give yourself permission to be protective. Your love will not only help keep your children from harm; it will build in them the confidence and spiritual backbone for living with integrity and leading others well.

TALK WITH YOUR SPOUSE ABOUT SETTING
THE APPROPRIATE BOUNDARIES FOR YOUR
CHILDREN REGARDING ACCESS TO THE
INTERNET, TELEVISION, MOVIES, AND PHONE
USE. PRAYERFULLY DRAW UP GUIDELINES FOR
WHAT KINDS OF ACTIVITIES ARE ALLOWABLE
WITH THEIR FRIENDS. BEFORE YOU PRESENT
YOUR DECISIONS TO THEM, PRAY FOR DIS-
CERNMENT AND FOR THE LORD TO WORK IN
BOTH YOUR AND YOUR CHILDREN'S HEARTS.

___ Check here when you've completed today's dare.

What did you decide? Did new areas come up as you prayed?
How did your children respond?

_____

_____

_____

_____

_____

_____

_____

_____

Like hovering birds, so the LORD of Hosts will protect Jerusalem—by protecting it,
He will rescue it, by sparing it, He will deliver it. (Isaiah 31:5 HCSB)

DAY 20
Love takes time

Be careful how you walk, not as unwise men but as wise,
making the most of your time. (Ephesians 5:15–16)

Imagine lying on your deathbed and looking back over your life. What would you wish you could have done more? Worked in the office? Cleaned the house? Watched more TV? No. Those things won't matter then. Often people's greatest regrets come from wishing they had loved more the people most important to them. But they never got around to it.

And if you're not careful, everything secondary and menial in your life will steal your time away from those you love. Just a few extra hours of work. Another business trip. Catching the last minutes of another game on television. One more e-mail, social media update, or viral video you feel tempted to check. You look up seconds later and wonder where the hours went, then where the years and your children went.

There's never enough time for it all. Everything will take as much time as you give it. Something always gets left out, but we must wisely choose what does . . . and what doesn't.

All your current work and sacrifice, you hope, is leading to a place where you'll eventually have freedom and some time with those you really love—one day out in the future, when you can finally stop and enjoy them. But what about enjoying them now? You don't have the future. All you really have is now. Regardless of what it is, if something always ends up keeping you away from your family, then is it such a good thing after all? Remember, the "good" is always the enemy of God's best. We must choose the best that's within our grasp.

Our children don't typically fuss when we come home late again or tell them we're currently busy. They end up waiting in the shadows until they get tired of our excuses and eventually move on to other things. Besides, we promise we'll make it up to them. Next weekend maybe. But what we're unknowingly shouting is, "We're busy with things that are really important. You're not. Go bother somebody else."

We would never *say* that, of course. But it may be what they hear. We would never run off and abandon our children all at once, yet we could be abandoning them by subtle, slow degrees, month after month, continually leaving them as sheep without a shepherd.

We are the ones who need to step in and press pause. Because love takes time. Precious, priceless time. It is the perpetual passing of our lives. It never waits and never returns. Every act of love requires it. To waste time is to waste a portion of life and another opportunity to love.

Scripture commands parents to prioritize time with their children. It is one of our most important responsibilities. The greatest commandment of all, premiering in Deuteronomy 6, is to "love the LORD your God" with everything you are (verse 5). This is the pinnacle imperative of God's laws. But the next two verses explain that parents must teach their children to love God through daily interaction with them in the morning, while sitting together at home, while we are out traveling, and around bedtime at night. These four key times are God's recipe to guide our priorities. Our children need us to carve out daily time for them so we can represent God and His priorities well.

Jesus exposed the true nature of the overly busy person while visiting in the home of His friends, Mary and Martha. He and His disciples' arrival meant, in Martha's mind, that she and her sister needed to work tirelessly with impressive preparations. Instead, she found Mary sitting at Jesus' feet, enjoying His company and hanging on every word.

"Lord," Martha interrupted, "do You not care that my sister has left me to do all the serving alone? Then tell her to help me." But Jesus, in His wise and gentle way, said, "Martha, Martha, you are worried and bothered about so many things; but only one thing is necessary, for Mary has chosen the good part, which shall not be taken away from her" (Luke 10:40–42).

His words soar through time and into our ears. *Quit worrying about secondary things. Choose the priority. Love on people while you can. Neglect the unnecessary.* It's what love does all the time. To choose our families over the busyness of the world is to choose the good part—the part that can never be "taken away." Love dares you to wield the powerful word "No" and use it liberally on things that will keep you from doing this.

Certainly there's a balance. Our kids should not be worshipped. God is first, our marriages second, and then our kids are third. Children, too, must wait sometimes. But everything below them needs to take a backseat in our hearts and find its proper place in our schedules while we guard our time with the ones God has entrusted to our care.

So push back against the tyranny of the trivial. Budget your family time first to help you say no to other things. Work hard when it's work time, then intentionally delegate or postpone the rest. Stop worrying about pleasing people who won't be crying at your funeral. Sacrifice the good for the best so you can daily put your love on display. Leave the dishes and the bushes a few more minutes. They'll still be there to tackle after you've spent a little extra time with your kids.

We can make impressive statements about what matters most to us, but our use of time will make the loudest and most accurate statement of all.

TODAY'S DARE

Turn off the television and Internet tonight and spend some focused quality time with your children. Talk, listen, and play with them.

___ Check here when you've completed today's dare.

What did you choose to do, and how did your family respond?

_____

_____

_____

_____

_____

_____

_____

_____

_____

_____

For "12 Daring Ideas to Maximize Family Time," see page 205 in the appendix.

She looks well to the ways of her household. (Proverbs 31:27)

DAY 21
Love is fair

There is no partiality with God. (Romans 2:11)

Favoritism almost always leads to envy, anger, and jealousy. And the last person seeing it is often the very person showing it. But to the child who's being made to feel less desirable, less capable, or less enjoyable to be around—they can sense favoritism the very moment it happens.

Our selfish, human nature is what causes us to give preference to the rich over the poor, the beautiful over the plain, and the strong over the weak. But this is not the nature of love. This is why God made a point of telling us He does not show partiality Himself (Romans 2:11) and that we, too, should do "nothing in a spirit of partiality" (1 Timothy 5:21).

He also communicated this principle in the Bible through powerful, true stories. The fact that most of these examples occur within the context of family warns us to especially avoid committing this troubling crime with our sons and daughters, even by perception.

When Jacob was tricked into marrying Leah instead of Rachel, his resulting favoritism of Rachel led to repeated rivalry and hurt feelings (Genesis 30:1–2). Later on, Jacob's favoritism toward Rachel's firstborn son, Joseph, led his other sons to want to kill their little brother (Genesis 37:18–20).

It was envy that drove a paranoid King Saul into rage and murderous plotting against David, the young man favored by the people to be the king's successor. Jealousy caused Jesus' followers to argue with each other over who would be the greatest. And if anything summarizes the Pharisees' hatred of Jesus, it was their envy of His power and authority as the crowds flocked to see Him teach and heal (Matthew 27:18).

The Scriptures warn, "Wrath is fierce and anger is a flood, but who can stand before jealousy?" (Proverbs 27:4). And if we are to love our children well, we must guard against its subtle and dangerous ability to infiltrate our families in at least two major ways:

1. *Jealousy among siblings.* You would never intentionally pit one child against another, but their young eyes pick up on everything you do, even the unintended. They can perceive the amount of time you give to one of them over another and any inconsistencies in the way you dish out discipline. They can recognize when you show more pleasure in one over another. They may not come out and say it, but the marks of discouragement and fading esteem could linger behind their eyes if you're not clearly balancing your love. This obscure resentment could later result in open rebellion.

Yes, certain seasons, schedules, or circumstances will require you to focus more on a particular child's needs—even their misbehaviors. Older children almost always get to do new things first. More assertive and responsible children are usually rewarded more readily. And submissive children are naturally less stressful and easier to be around than a strong-willed, defiant child.

But in each situation, love drives us to work hard to shepherd each of their insecure hearts, value their strengths, and guide our words with wisdom to help us eliminate any weed of envy that wants to take root inside them.

To do this, you must make sure every little heart hears, sees, and feels your personal love. Every child needs consistent, affectionate, one-on-one time with each parent. Otherwise, the perception you leave will be the reality they believe.

2. *Jealousy among parents.* Both mom and dad possess different gifts, personalities, and roles. And God intends to use each of us differently to more fully meet our children's needs. But this tag-team transaction is not always an even trade. One of you is more often likely to be the "fun parent." One may discipline more harshly. One seems to have easier responsibilities. And this can lead to one or both of you feeling jealous and angry at the other.

But remember, love is patient, kind, and unselfish. It celebrates success instead of being threatened by it. You must both intercept any potential envy by frequently, deliberately thanking God for the qualities in your spouse that make them such a good parent. Tell them so. When praying together, thank God often for the shared partnership you enjoy in working as one to help your children become complete individuals. If one child favors you, then praise their other parent and help lead your child's heart to understand and value them more.

Lastly, the most fertile ground where jealousy and partiality can take root is in blended families and split custody situations. You may live in this dynamic and understand that "jealousy" issues don't always have easy answers. But that doesn't mean these situations cannot be averted and minimized. You must apply patience liberally. Always be complimentary, not critical, of people who aren't in the room. Respond quickly in overwhelming love to any child who appears threatened. Try not to let old wounds leak into present-day preferences. Don't give jealousy even one square inch to thrive in your home.

Our children will always have a hard time receiving our love if they perceive it's second-rate in comparison to our love for others. But genuine love, often and freely expressed, can help put out the fires that envy wants to set. Give your children the joyful heart that's found in your well-balanced love.

SET UP A SPECIAL BOX OR FOLDER FOR
EACH OF YOUR CHILDREN. BEGIN COLLECTING
KEEPSAKES, PHOTOS, AWARDS, AND MEMORIES.
LET THEM KNOW YOU'LL BE CONTINUING
TO GATHER NEW THINGS SPECIAL TO THEM.
OCCASIONALLY GO THROUGH THEIR BOX
WITH THEM AS A WAY OF EXPRESSING
HOW PROUD YOU ARE OF THEIR
LIFE AND ACHIEVEMENTS.

___ Check here when you've completed today's dare.

What way did you choose for affirming each of your children
equally? What do you think it meant and will mean to them?

_____

_____

_____

_____

_____

_____

_____

Be of the same mind toward one another. (Romans 12:16)

DAY 22
Love honors authority

Listen to your father who begot you, and do not despise
your mother when she is old. (Proverbs 23:22)

Few things are more pleasant in a child than seeing them
honor authority. Paying attention to their teachers. Following
the instructions of their coaches. Showing courtesy to their
elders. Perhaps most of all, seeing them look into the eyes of
their parents with loving respect and obedience.

There is one primary command in the Bible addressed specifically to kids: "Children, obey your parents in the Lord, for
this is right" (Ephesians 6:1). But greater than merely helping
them be pleasant, God has promised lifelong rewards to those
who honor their parents. And love's job is to help your children
understand this vital truth.

Of the ten commandments Moses brought down off the
mountain, God singled out the fifth commandment—"Honor
your father and mother"—by giving it perhaps His most
ringing endorsement and motivation: "so that it may be well
with you, and that you may live long on the earth" (Ephesians
6:2–3). Something special happens when children recognize
the core importance of God's ordained authority structure. It
contributes to their overall sense of well-being. It also sets the
tone for receiving greater trust, freedom, and blessing from
their parents, and invites God's blessing as well.

That's why love so desperately wants this for our children.
Not just to make life easier on *us*, but to enable them to walk an
entire lifetime under the continued favor of God.

In contrast, many tragedies in the lives of young people
often result from rebellion against their parents. How ironic

that those who complain the most about the pain and dysfunction in their lives are often the same ones who resisted the counsel their parents gave them over the years. But they turned a deaf ear to it and are living with the consequences.

What happens with your children at home will follow them everywhere. By training them to speak respectfully to you, obey without complaint, and work as hard when they're alone as when they're being overseen, you are equipping them to honor and win the favor of all future authorities in their lives. Most important, this prepares them to more quickly obey God as He speaks and reveals His wonderful plans to them.

No, they won't do everything perfectly. Neither do we. But we need to help them understand that God, in His perfection, intentionally uses imperfect authorities to carry out His perfect will. The Bible says all authority comes from Him. And regardless if it is family, government officials, church leaders, or employers, our authorities have been established to represent His protective and guiding rule over us (Romans 13:1–4).

Unless such authorities are asking us to sin, we are to honor God by honoring them and their instructions. We may disagree and respectfully appeal to a specific decision, but we are not to gain or entertain a heart of rebellion against them.

God values authority so highly, He made it a frequent part of His teaching throughout the Bible. In the Old Testament, children in Israel who hurt or cursed their parents were given the same punishment as those who committed murder or blasphemed God (Exodus 21:15–17).

After the coming of Christ, God still instructed believers to distinguish themselves by the honorable way they acted toward those in leadership positions—even if those people were heartless and cruel. While the world scoffs at unsympathetic authorities, Christ-followers are to be set apart by their continued respect. Jesus said, "Whoever forces you to go one mile, go with him two" (Matthew 5:41). The Scripture says, "Be submissive to your masters with all respect, not only to those who are good and gentle, but also to those who are unreasonable" (1 Peter 2:18). God tells us to pray for "all who are in authority" over us (1 Timothy 2:1–2).

Respect them. Honor them. Serve them. Pray for them. Even those who take advantage of their superiority over you. The Christian's willingness to perform their duties beyond what is asked of them shines a spotlight on what Christ's power and love have brought about in their hearts.

Your children will need you to teach them at home the wisdom of humbling themselves before authority. "Obey your leaders and submit to them," the Bible says, so that your authorities can fulfill their responsibilities "with joy and not with grief" (Hebrews 13:17).

Now, ask yourself if *honor* is the attitude toward authority your kids see in you? When you pass a patrolman? When you talk about government leadership? When you mention what your boss is like? When the pastor makes a decision you don't fully understand? When you interact with your own parents and are called on to care for their aging needs?

We not only need to watch our tones; we need to check our hearts. Before we buck someone's authority, are we aware that God is the one responsible for placing that person in their position of leadership over us? Are we praying for them? Are we concerned about their welfare? Their soul? Do we want them to see the light of Jesus in us? If we want our children to live in the blessings of respecting our parental authority, love calls us to set the example and lead the way.

REFLECT ON YOUR OWN ATTITUDES
ABOUT AUTHORITY IN YOUR LIFE. IF THE
LORD EXPOSES ANY WRONGDOING IN YOUR
HEART, CONFESS IT AND ASK FORGIVENESS.
TALK WITH YOUR CHILDREN ABOUT THE
IMPORTANCE OF HONORING GOD BY
HONORING THEIR AUTHORITIES.

___ Check here when you've completed today's dare.

What did the Lord reveal to you, and what was your response?

There is no authority except from God, and those
which exist are established by God. (Romans 13:1)

DAY 23
Love intercedes

My house will be called a house of prayer. (Isaiah 56:7)

The more children grow, the more unpredictable their lives become. More opportunities for slip-ups and letdowns. More chances for the wrong people to whisper backward thinking in their ears. More ways for their decisions to turn around and bite them. No matter how smart or savvy you may be, your children are still subject to circumstances and surprises beyond your reach. You cannot always protect them or control the flow around their lives.

But love has a stellar battle strategy and backup plan.

It's called PRAYER.

God understands and loves your children more than you do. He can see your kids when you do not. He can go with them, watch over them, and guide them where you cannot. And He invites you to place them and your every other concern into His loving arms.

His Word tells us . . .

"Pour out your heart before Him . . ." (Psalm 62:8).

"Ask, and it will be given to you . . ." (Matthew 7:7 NIV).

"If you then, being evil, know how to give good gifts to your children, how much more will your Father who is in heaven give what is good to those who ask Him!" (Matthew 7:11 NIV).

What a glorious, gracious God He is! We are not only invited into His throne room; we are expected to pray. Anytime about anything (1 Thessalonians 5:16–18). There is nothing more powerful you can do to greatly impact your children for good than to get on your knees and sincerely pray for them.

But prayer is not merely a response to our children's current crisis; it is an opportunity to talk to God on a regular basis about every area of their lives. From our lips to His ears, we should often pray *for* them, *with* them, and *around* them.

God is not our servant, but He lovingly allows prayer to influence Him and change things. Consider this: prayer can accomplish what a willing God can accomplish. Powerfully and effectively (James 5:16).

But there are keys to doing it right. Scripture says that for our prayers to be unhindered, we must know God (John 14:6), be right with Him (Psalm 66:18), be right with others (Mark 11:22–26; 1 Peter 3:7), and have our hearts right, in humility and faith (James 1:5–8; 4:6). Then, by virtue of the access to God that Jesus Christ attained for us through His sacrifice on the cross, we can "draw near with confidence to the throne of grace, so that we may receive mercy and find grace to help in time of need" (Hebrews 4:16).

By uniting our hearts with Him and keeping our thoughts and desires aligned with His in prayer, we place ourselves in a position to bring about more good for our children than anything else we could do on earth (John 15:7).

In prayer, we gain more of His insight and wisdom into their lives and needs. We can lovingly request that He will protect and provide for them, bloom and bless them, guard and guide them. Our intercession allows us to stand in the gap against evil and temptation and ask God to save and strengthen them. In prayer, we can join Him in waging war (Ephesians 6:10–19) against the spiritual forces that would "steal and kill and destroy" their dreams and futures (John 10:10).

But not only does prayer defend them; it also positively impacts them. More effective than our prodding, the regular prayer in our home draws them closer to God while drawing their attention away from their problems and onto the One who holds every answer. Your words of thanksgiving to God will remind them of His faithfulness. Then as He responds to your requests, your children will get to see His handiwork firsthand.

Taking our kids with us into prayer leads them toward respecting God, but also to the hope and confidence that He can provide everything they need to live for Him.

If you don't know what to pray about, then consider what you are currently worried about. Your worries are merely burdens you are bearing in your own strength that you haven't yet cast fully upon God's strength (Philippians 4:6–7).

"Therefore humble yourselves under the mighty hand of God, that He may exalt you at the proper time, casting all your anxiety on Him, because He cares for you" (1 Peter 5:6–7).

If a Bible verse leaps from the page as you read it, fold it into your prayer strategy for each of your kids. Personalize it to their needs. More specific requests get more specific answers. If you desire great things, then ask for great things. Launch the ball into God's court and see how He responds. But don't let things lack and fail simply because you lacked to pray and failed to ask (James 4:2).

Prayer is a language of love. We should speak it as naturally as breathing. With the same regularity as driving our kids to school or asking how their day went, we can deal with any issue that arises in their lives by praying about it.

So train your children to be wise and careful, but trust your children to the One who ultimately holds their success and safety in His omnipotent hands (Psalm 127:1–2). Prayer lets your love soar to new heights so your heart can rest under the shadow of the Almighty.

LOOK OVER THE APPENDIX SECTIONS ABOUT
PRAYER AT THE END OF THIS BOOK. USE SOME
OF THE ITEMS LISTED IN "HOW TO PRAY FOR
YOUR CHILDREN" (PAGE 208) AS A SPRING-
BOARD TO BEGIN PRAYING FOR YOUR KIDS.
AFTER TALKING WITH GOD ON THEIR BEHALF,
SHARE WITH YOUR CHILDREN WHAT YOU ARE
NOW PRAYING FOR THEIR LIVES.

___ Check here when you've completed today's dare.

In what areas did the Lord lead you to pray for your children?

This is the confidence which we have before Him, that,
if we ask anything according to His will, He hears us. (1 John 5:14)

DAY 24
Love forgives

If you forgive others for their transgressions,
your heavenly Father will also forgive you. (Matthew 6:14)

As long as there are muddy feet, sibling rivalry, and a variety of uses for the living room furniture, parents will always have plenty of opportunities to practice the fine art of forgiveness.

But if not for love, we'll use these opportunities for other things, like displaying our vocal volume, declaring the nearness of our martyrdom, and preserving pain in our memories. Instead of letting our kids see what being forgiven feels like, we'll leave the impression that love can only go so far before it runs out of gas and can't take it anymore.

Too often we focus on enforcing justice. We come down hard or throw our child into a prison of our own anger. And though our job is to teach them that actions come with consequences, the equally priceless quest of parenting is to show them that "love covers a multitude of sins" (1 Peter 4:8).

When we discipline our children, the end game is not only to obtain an admission of guilt and change of direction, but to look them in the eye with restorative love and assure them we forgive them for breaking our trust or violating our rules . . . again. We are grieved by what they've done, but we still love them and choose to release them—not from punishment or a temporary loss of privilege, but from any lingering anger and tension between us. We will take the lead in reestablishing the relationship after a painful breach.

That's how love endures. It remembers Jesus' words— "Blessed are the merciful, for they shall receive mercy," and

"Blessed are the peacemakers, for they shall be called sons of God" (Matthew 5:7, 9). Love knows that the day we stop forgiving is the day that we poison our own hearts with bitterness and spiral our relationship with our children downward toward ongoing anger and isolation. It knows that lasting love and unforgiveness cannot coexist for very long in the same heart or home. One will always force the other out.

Love knows how to put on a thickness of armor that is hard to offend, and then it gives us wisdom to confront another's crimes with grace. It willingly works to bring everyone back to the table. And it knows life is too short to let the past keep poisoning the fellowship of the future.

When anyone refuses to forgive, bitterness will bloom, hearts will harden, and the affectionate feelings of tenderness will fade into the background. And so love reminds us to release our anger, reach out, and restore. We must keep forgiving our children as we have been forgiven (Ephesians 4:32; Matthew 18:22).

But that's not the only way our forgiveness can make a deep imprint on our children's hearts. They know, for example, when Mom and Dad aren't getting along. They are watching how you work things out and what marital mercy looks like. They overhear you talk about coworkers, dysfunctional neighbors, and people who are conveniently making things hard on you. They learn your extended family's epic saga of who did what to whom, and why you intentionally never get around to seeing certain relatives at holidays anymore.

Your children are seeing and learning. And they are either discovering how they should dig in their heels and find a reason to remain bitter, or how to extend the loving grace that God extends to us, and then overcoming their greatest obstacles with forgiveness and peacemaking.

What if your kids routinely saw you tackle relational train wrecks with relentless love? What if they watched you end every chilly stalemate with your spouse by apologizing or extending heartfelt patience and compassion?

Then they would vividly see the power of love in action. They would learn one of the greatest secrets to forever friendships and monumental marriages. They would know when you look them in the eye and say, "I forgive you," you absolutely mean it. And even if the subject of their childish offense was to surface again in conversation, it would be as a point of instruction, not as fuel for a fight or a rebounding of outdated anger.

Yes, forgiveness is best when triggered by another's repentance (Luke 17:3). This is healthy and good for everybody—the beautiful hope of full-circle restoration. But regardless of what others do, Jesus said our forgiveness must stay unconditional (Mark 11:25–26) and never-ending (Matthew 18:21–22), knowing that our spiritual lives will always be impacted by it (Matthew 6:14–15). We can still forgive knowing that God is the true judge and avenger of all (Romans 12:19), and that any root of bitterness we allow to remain in our hearts will only fester, pollute, and poison us (Hebrews 12:15).

Forgiveness is not always sweet and gentle. It can be very hard to do. But the more it is practiced and becomes your go-to reflex, the easier and more automatic it becomes.

When you forgive your children for their mistakes—both the petty and the paramount ones—you are handing down an incredible example for them to one day extend to a hundred other relationships. You're even contributing to the lives of your grandchildren, who will more likely be raised knowing there's always a place for them within their parents' heart and home, no matter what—just like your love proved to your own.

TODAY'S DARE

SEARCH YOUR HEART FOR ANY UNRESOLVED ANGER OR UNFORGIVENESS AGAINST YOUR CHILDREN (OR ANYONE ELSE, FOR THAT MATTER). WRITE DOWN THEIR NAMES AND A LIST OF THEIR OFFENSES. PRAY FOR THEM AND ASK GOD TO GIVE YOU THE LOVE AND GRACE TO FORGIVE THEM. THEN CROSS OUT WHAT THEY HAVE DONE WITH PERMANENT INK AND SAY ALOUD AND FROM YOUR HEART, "I CHOOSE TO FORGIVE YOU." THROW THE PAPER AWAY AS A TESTAMENT TO YOUR FORGIVENESS AND NEWFOUND FREEDOM.

___ Check here when you've completed today's dare.

How do you feel after choosing to forgive? What did God do in your heart?

_____

_____

_____

_____

_____

_____

_____

Who is this who even forgives sins? (Luke 7:49 NKJV)

DAY 25
Love takes responsibility

The one who conceals his sins will not prosper, but whoever confesses and renounces them will find mercy. (Proverbs 28:13 HCSB)

Most parents know how to teach their kids to apologize properly. To look their mother or little brother in the eye and say "I was wrong and I'm sorry." *And mean it.*

But it's also important for us as parents to live out this lecture whenever *we* are in the wrong. One of the most powerful experiences that strengthens the bond of mutual honor between a parent and child is when a mom or dad steps up and says to their children, "No, I'm the one at fault here and need to apologize to you. Will you please forgive me?" This may seem counterproductive to maintaining a child's respect. But it is actually fundamental to guarding and growing it.

During their formative years, our children are slow to pick up on our flaws. We daily define reality for them and usually paint ourselves in a positive light. We also become the go-to gurus for all their problems. As a result, they tend to put us on a pedestal and assume we have it all together.

But then we stumble and fall. Time reveals our humanity. Our children start feeling the aftershocks of our sinfulness and inconsistency.

Sometimes, for example, we're guilty of not thinking ahead. We cram too much into the day and kick out the very activity our child was counting on. Sometimes we just aren't careful. They wholeheartedly speak, but we're only half-listening. Sometimes we're forgetful or lazy. Self-centered or angry. Ungrateful. Sinful.

But that's when love reminds us that there are no perfect parents—just the prideful, self-righteous ones who live in denial, and humble, honest ones who take responsibility for their mistakes. Love soberly invites us to look our children in the eye and tell them the truth about our brokenness (without some of the gory details). To embrace the benefits of repentance, owning up to what we've done and adjusting our course.

Why is this important? Because love brings healing to hurts. It won't hide behind hypocritical masks. It is willingly accountable. It "rejoices with the truth" (1 Corinthians 13:6) and treasures honesty as a trademark.

All parents need to become aware that a list of their crimes is probably being compiled over time in the hearts of their children. Wrongs they perceive that you have done. Hurtful words. Broken promises. Angry outbursts. Times when you have not practiced what you preached.

The older your kids grow, the more this list can become detrimental to your parenting. The devil will use it to whisper accusations in their ears against you. Each item can become a seed that helps them plant more anger toward you. To push your heart away. To justify future rebellion. Love, however, "keeps no record of wrongs" (1 Corinthians 13:5 NIV), so you must help your child work through and eliminate this list.

But first, you must find out what is on it. Simply go to them and ask, "Are you upset with me for any reason? Have I hurt you and never made it right? Have I ever made a promise and didn't keep it? Are there things you feel I have done wrong that we have never talked about or worked through?"

Then get ready to write. You must help your son or daughter deal with each issue through your humble confession or your honest clarification. As they share with you, some things may seem very petty or easily explainable, but take each item seriously. Instead of arguing over details, start by thanking them for their openness, and then honestly apologize for anything they mentioned where you know you may not have done the right or loving thing.

It takes only a few seconds to sincerely say, "I'm sorry," and ask your children to forgive you, but it can retie your hearts together and transform your relationship with them for years to come.

Confession is *courageous*. It deals with issues head-on. If parents don't learn to make the truth their best friend in these situations, then it will become their worst enemy. We must help our children stay completely free from bitterness against us by taking responsibility for our part in wronging them.

Second, we should *concrete* our confessions. We must commit to exemplifying a life that lines up with our words, not only until the temperature in the house comes back down, but with ongoing, prayerful dependence on God. We're not just confessing; we're changing.

Last, we should be careful to *clarify* any situations they mentioned where we were not actually in the wrong. This will help them clear their minds of doubts and worries they may have been harboring against us.

A wise parent must realign expectations with reality. It never hurts to say to them, "I really want to be a good parent, but I make a lot of mistakes. I need God's forgiveness daily and I will need yours daily too. If you ever feel I have wronged you in any way, please come to me so we can talk it through."

By learning to show us mercy, our kids will develop the habit of being merciful. In this way, we help them learn first-hand how to cradle important but strained relationships in their hands and still hold them together. It's forgiveness: the home improvement edition.

TODAY'S DARE

ASK GOD TO HELP YOU MODEL
RESPONSIBLE LOVE TO YOUR CHILDREN.
USING THE QUESTIONS MENTIONED IN THIS
CHAPTER, GO TO EACH CHILD AND ASK IF YOU
HAVE HURT OR WRONGED THEM IN ANY WAY.
BE READY TO LISTEN AND HUMBLY APOLOGIZE
FOR ANYTHING YOU MAY HAVE DONE WRONG
OR TO CLARIFY ISSUES WHERE THEY MAY HAVE
MISUNDERSTOOD YOUR ACTIONS. ASK THEM
TO FORGIVE YOU, AND THANK THEM FOR
THEIR HONESTY AND COMPASSION.

___ Check here when you've completed today's dare.

What happened when you talked with your children? What
came up that you were not expecting? How did you respond?
How did *they* respond?

_____

_____

_____

_____

_____

_____

_____

I acknowledged my sin to You and did not conceal my iniquity. (Psalm 32:5 HCSB)

DAY 26
Love is Jesus Christ

By this the love of God was manifested in us,
that God has sent His only begotten Son into the world
so that we might live through Him. (1 John 4:9)

Of all the things love leads us to do as parents, nothing is more important than leading our children's hearts into a real and living relationship with God. *Nothing!* We cannot say we've given them everything we can give them until we've introduced them to the greatest love of all and shown them how Jesus Christ can give them true peace with God.

You may not have come to this book knowing God on a personal level yourself. You may not have found His forgiveness by entrusting your life to Him and accepting Christ's loving sacrifice for you on the cross.

If that is true, then you are not reading this by accident.

At the deepest levels of our mutual love for our children is a desire to understand and teach them what really matters most in life. And when everything else is stripped away, one thing remains as the most important—God created us and our children with an eternal purpose in mind: to become His children, to know His love, to honor Him with our lives, and to spend an eternity with Him (John 3:16).

This is why the Son of God came to earth Himself as a newborn baby. He was "born of a woman, born under the Law, so that He might redeem those who were under the Law, that we might receive the adoption as sons" (Galatians 4:4–5) . . . so that He "might free those who through fear of death were subject to slavery all their lives" (Hebrews 2:15).

Surely you have had some experience with feeling enslaved to sin and tasting the fear of death. We all know we are imperfect. We don't have all the answers. We all know we will die someday. God alone holds the mysteries of what lies beyond the grave, and He promises that He will judge us there for the things we have done on earth (Romans 14:10–12).

As the Bible says, "Having overlooked the times of ignorance, God is now declaring to men that all people everywhere should repent, because He has fixed a day in which He will judge the world in righteousness" (Acts 17:30–31).

But find rest in the fact that you and your children can experience lifelong, eternal freedom from guilt, fear, hopelessness, and shame. The person you're working so hard to shape your kids into from the outside can be blessed, transformed, and energized by God's love and power on the inside.

Only one truth leads to this certainty: the truth that more than two thousand years ago, a man named Jesus of Nazareth, God's Son, walked in human perfection and willingly shed His blood for us. The Bible explains that His birth was unique, His life fulfilled hundreds of prophecies, His teaching revealed eternal truth, His love was unexcelled, and His sacrificial death on a Roman cross was perfect and complete. He came to take the punishment we deserve, and He paid the price that each of us owes a holy God to take away our guilt.

Because of Christ, we and our children are invited by God to turn from our sins, call upon the name of Jesus, and place our faith in Him (Romans 10:13). You are invited to "confess with your mouth Jesus as Lord, and believe in your heart that God raised Him from the dead" (Romans 10:9). By opening your heart to Him, His promise to you is as simple as it is profound and secure: "You will be saved." And it comes with a lifetime promise: "Whoever believes in Him will not be disappointed" (Romans 10:11). You receive undeserved forgiveness. Real peace and hope. A relationship with God and eternal life right now, continuing on beyond death and the grave.

That's how much God loves you.

That's how much He loves your children.

You don't need to understand everything about God to reach out to Him and trust Him. You don't have to know it all to share His love with your kids. The Lord has loved them from "before the foundation of the world" (Ephesians 1:4 HCSB), but in His love, He graciously invites you to participate with Him at every step along their way.

A child should never be pressured into making any type of spiritual decision before they're ready. Hurrying them along usually only leads them to resent it later rather than truly embrace it and live it. So parents should focus on modeling God's love for their children, praying for their salvation, and patiently planting seeds of truth about Jesus into their hearts. At some point in your child's life, God can help them realize they are imperfect and sinful, in need of His forgiveness.

As He stirs their hearts, God will then open up doors of conversation and give you the privilege of showing them how to turn to Him and freely place their hearts into His hands. At that moment, He will place His Spirit into theirs. This is one of the greatest joys in life and the highest priorities of parenting.

When they do trust Him and begin growing in faith, you can make a point of regularly showing them how life with Jesus can bless every aspect of who they are. The work He does in their hearts will keep guiding them, strengthening them, and restoring them toward a rich lifetime of joy and meaning.

Jesus is what their hearts need more than anything else. Helping them to know Him and follow Him daily should be an ongoing focus of your prayers and your loving encouragement.

ASK YOURSELF IF YOU HAVE TRULY TRUSTED CHRIST AS SAVIOR AND LORD. IF SO, SPEND TIME THANKING HIM FOR HIS PRICELESS GIFT. IF NOT, YOU CAN SETTLE THIS QUESTION TODAY BY TURNING FROM YOUR SIN AND ASKING FOR HIS FORGIVENESS AND SALVATION. THEN SHARE HIS TRUTH AND YOUR STORY WITH YOUR CHILDREN.

___ Check here when you've completed today's dare.

Where are you in your walk of faith? Where are your children? Have you ever taken time to fully share your faith journey with them? If you are unsure whether or not you are truly saved, consider reading the short book of 1 John near the end of your Bible for clarity or assurance.

For more about how to understand, experience, and share God's salvation with your children, turn to page 214 in the appendix: "How to Find Peace with God."

You therefore, my son, be strong in the grace that is in Christ Jesus. (2 Timothy 2:1 NKJV)

DAY 27
Love is satisfied in God

He has satisfied the thirsty soul, and the hungry soul
He has filled with what is good. (Psalm 107:9 NIV)

God didn't give us children so we could lose ourselves in them, using them as our new source of identity and meaning. Nor did He intend for us to palm them off on others while we go searching for fulfillment elsewhere.

God Himself wants to be our chief source of satisfaction. The vacuum that's left inside us by our selfishness and fallenness cannot be fulfilled by anything else but Him.

People often think if they had more money, pleasure, or power, they could be happy. King Solomon attained all these things in great measure and discovered that "all was vanity and striving after wind" (Ecclesiastes 2:1–25). He finally concluded that since all good things ultimately come from God's hand, "who can have enjoyment without Him?" (verse 25).

Yet whenever we feel low on happiness, we tend to think it's found in some thing we want but don't have. We don't realize that God did not create things on earth that will satisfy us more than He does—even our children. He formed the longings within us so we would seek Him and be filled with His heavenly supply (Philippians 4:19). True love, joy, and peace are found only in close fellowship with Him (Galatians 5:22).

The Bible reveals that when we chase fulfillment in this world, we will miss it and miss God too. But when we find our sufficiency in God, we not only get God, but He also gives us true joy as gravy on the side. The psalmist said, "Delight yourself in the LORD; and He will give you the desires of your heart" (Psalm 37:4). When you are seeking and loving Him as your top priority, He promises to furnish your heart with exactly what you truly need and want.

Everybody in your home will benefit from a parent who's fully enjoying their relationship with God. When you begin to surrender control and let God fill you with His love, with renewed purpose, and with a conscience at peace, then the joy welling up inside you will begin pouring out onto the people in your family as well.

That's why it wasn't insensitive of Jesus to say, "He who loves son or daughter more than Me is not worthy of Me" (Matthew 10:37). As counterintuitive as this statement may sound, your kids really *shouldn't* come first in life's pecking order. Neither should your spouse or even yourself.

One of the great dares of parental love is to plug all your passions into the channel of fellowship with God, then watch Him empower and multiply what your love is able to accomplish in your kids' lives—much more than you could ever produce before. Loving God first will enable you to love your children even better.

That's why it can be said: *Living in satisfying fellowship with Him is truly the secret to dynamic parenting.*

This doesn't mean becoming indifferent to your children's needs. But it does mean that by staying connected to God in prayer each day and looking to Him for wisdom and strength, He will develop a sensitivity in you concerning their most important needs.

His Holy Spirit will be constantly pouring God's love into your heart (Romans 5:1–5). He will be giving you peace to sustain you in uncertain circumstances when your own willpower would run out of steam. He will be instilling His joy in you that transcends any situation, no matter how bad it can be.

That's the beauty of being satisfied in Him. Circumstances become irrelevant because He and His promises never change. So by making yourself available for Him to fill and use, your children won't be shortchanged. Quite the opposite. What they receive will have been poured through you directly from the heart of God and into theirs.

Sometimes in life, your kids may actually need less of you. You may be doing too much for them out of fear or an unhealthy desire to find your validity in them. In other places, they may need more than what you can possibly give. But in God, you will be constantly prepared by His Spirit to serve them in whatever way is best. God's Word, wisdom, and patience will simply start coming out of you because of what you're allowing Him to place inside you every day.

Jacob's wife Leah (Genesis 29:30–35) serves as an example of someone who expected to find full satisfaction in her family. Unloved by her husband, she hoped that having children would endear her to his heart. She bore him three sons, giving each of them names that expressed her longing for contentment and security. But she eventually found that no person could carry the weight of her deepest emotional and spiritual needs. When her fourth son was born, she simply said, "This time I will praise the LORD" (verse 35). She ended her search where each of ours needs to begin. In loving God.

We should take our hearts to God when we feel unsatisfied. And because His vast, unending abundance is able to "satisfy the desire of every living thing" (Psalm 145:16), we don't need to worry one second that His supply won't be enough.

"In Your presence is fullness of joy," King David wrote in praise of the Lord. "In Your right hand there are pleasures forever" (Psalm 16:11). You can enjoy God as your everyday source. Of everything you need.

TODAY'S DARE

READ JESUS' WORDS FROM MATTHEW 11:28–30.
SPEND TIME WITH GOD AND ASK HIM HOW
YOU CAN DAILY FIND REST IN HIM. OPEN UP
YOUR HEART AND ASK HIM TO FILL YOU
WITH HIS LOVE AND TO HELP YOU FIND YOUR
HEART'S DELIGHT THROUGH A MORE
INTIMATE WALK WITH HIM. THANK HIM FOR
HIS GOODNESS AND PROVISION IN YOUR LIFE.
ENJOY YOUR TIME BEING CENTERED ON HIM.
THEN LET YOUR KIDS SEE THE DIFFERENCE
THIS MAKES IN YOU TODAY.

___ Check here when you've completed today's dare.

What changes in your life and attitudes will help you become
more satisfied in God alone? What did He reveal to you? How
will this benefit your children?

_____

_____

_____

_____

_____

_____

_____

I am at rest in God alone; my salvation comes from Him. (Psalm 62:1 HCSB)

DAY 28
Love is God's Word

We will not conceal them from their children, but tell to the generation to come the praises of the LORD. (Psalm 78:4)

"So great is my veneration for the Bible," said John Quincy Adams, sixth president of the United States, "that the earlier my children begin to read it, the more confident will be my hope that they will prove useful citizens of their country and respectable members of society."

All parents should discover this. Children who hear the truths of the Bible, who read it, and who hide it in their hearts and minds are much more readily equipped for life. They will hold inside themselves the counsel of God on subjects ranging from honesty and fairness to health and money management. From workplace ethics to servant leadership. They will better understand the foundational cornerstones for building greater marriages, families, businesses, governments, and societies. They will become well versed in faith, the nature of God, and the meaning of history and eternity. Most important, they will hear and become more acquainted with the voice of God. Spending time in the Bible can do all of that and more.

Yet this important course of childhood education does not require parents who are spiritual geniuses or hold seminary degrees. It starts with a mom or dad who simply love their children, love their God, love His Word, and are willing to help their kids develop a rich appetite for the spiritual feast that is inside of it.

Too many parents think they must come up with a perfect plan before they can crack open a Bible around their children. But Christians are never left alone to grasp the major themes of

Scripture. If you know Christ, you have the Holy Spirit within your heart as an illuminator of truth. "For the Spirit searches all things, even the depths of God" (1 Corinthians 2:10). And because of His internal lamp, the Scriptures are now yours to read, comprehend, live by, and share.

God loves your children without measure, and He will take responsibility for speaking to them through His Word if you just make sure they consistently hear it in church and in your home. It's not a matter of training and knowledge, but of willingness and love.

So start there. Don't sweat this. We encourage you to start in Genesis, or Proverbs, or the book of Matthew, and simply begin reading a chapter at a time out loud to your family sometime in the morning, at a meal, or before you go to bed at night.

There is no set formula. The Word will do the work, because it is "living and active and sharper than any two-edged sword" (Hebrews 4:12). As you read and discuss and pray over what you have read, your children will grow spiritually . . . and exponentially.

This idea may seem radical or revolutionary to you. Your schedule may not seem to allow time for it every day. But we dare you to join thousands of other families who have made the habit of Bible reading at home the most powerful moments in their week. It can become a lasting, memorable legacy in your children's lives. God's presence and power show up consistently in homes and hearts that choose to honor His Word.

This job is not too big for you. In fact, you are perfectly positioned and qualified—like no one else in the world—to lead your children through this treasure chest of spiritual gold, day after day. Opening your copy of the Bible before them is like unfolding a love letter and a treasure map, where each page marks another measure of the timeless ways and wonders of God, and where every exploration takes your whole family somewhere rich and new.

Hearing the Bible will allow your children to discover the morality of Moses, the faith of Abraham, the wisdom of Solomon, the passion of King David, and the lessons and love of Jesus Christ. Most of all, the sovereignty and providence of God throughout history will unfold within their hearts in relevant, living color. They will discover the Bible to be "more desirable than gold, yes, than much fine gold; sweeter also than honey and the drippings of the honeycomb" (Psalm 19:10).

If you could sit down and tell your children everything you know, you could only take them so far. Yet by daily placing the Word before them, "inspired by God and profitable for teaching, for rebuking, for correcting, for training in righteousness," you ensure that you are helping them become "complete, equipped for every good work" (2 Timothy 3:16–17 HCSB).

You can then approach your children at any time of crisis or decision in the future, and be able to say with confidence, "Continue in the things which you have learned and been assured of, knowing from whom you have learned them, and that from childhood you have known the Holy Scriptures, which are able to make you wise for salvation" (2 Timothy 3:14–15 NKJV).

Jesus said, "Everyone who hears these words of Mine and acts on them, may be compared to a wise man who built his house on the rock. The rain fell, and the floods came, and the winds blew and slammed against that house; and yet it did not fall, for it had been founded on the rock" (Matthew 7:24–25).

When your family is founded on the rock of God's unchanging Word, it is equipped, solid, and ensured for the storms and adventures of life.

TODAY'S DARE

IF YOU HAVE NOT BEEN HAVING A CONSISTENT TIME OF FAMILY DEVOTIONS, COMMIT TO STARTING THIS SPIRITUAL HABIT TODAY. IT CAN BE AS SIMPLE AS READING A SHORT PASSAGE, STORY, OR CHAPTER FROM SCRIPTURE. MAKE IT AN INTERACTIVE, REGULAR ADVENTURE IN YOUR HOME. IF YOU ALREADY DO THIS, PRAY SPECIFICALLY TODAY FOR GOD TO USE THESE MOMENTS TO SPEAK HIS TRUTH EVEN MORE CLEARLY AND POWERFULLY TO YOU AND YOUR KIDS.

___ Check here when you've completed today's dare.

Have you helped your children develop an appetite for the Word of God? Do you read it on a consistent basis? When is the best time in the day for you to lead a time of devotions in your home? Are there less important things that should take a back seat in your schedule so you can do this?

For a list of great verses to memorize with your children, see page 219 in the appendix.

One generation shall praise Your works to another,
and shall declare Your mighty acts. (Psalm 145:4)

DAY 29
Love listens

Father, I thank You that You have heard Me.
I knew that You always hear Me. (John 11:41–42)

Do your children believe that you truly understand them? How in tune are you to their concerns right now? Do you know their highest hopes and deepest fears? Do they feel comfortable telling you their secrets?

Of all the things our children need, regular moments of our undivided attention are near the top of the list. Deliberate, undistracted listening reminds them they matter to us.

So this makes parental attentiveness a priceless art form we must master as loving moms and dads. While multitasking is a necessity in this digital age, good listening requires us to pause and focus with a one-track mind. TV and earphones off. Computers and cell phones out of sight. Hands at rest, lips smiling, ears listening, and head nodding. Despite all our busyness, love must be allowed to interrupt us, inviting us to intentionally and consistently enter our children's world.

Everyone longs to experience a level of intimate friendship with others—to be "fully known and fully loved." It has been said that another pronunciation for the word *intimacy* is "into me you see," because this truly describes what happens when someone allows another person to know the deepest, darkest secrets of their heart. When they are freed to do this, assured they will still be accepted and loved even in this vulnerable position, a wonderful bonding experience occurs. People will always feel lonely inside if no one truly knows them and loves them at the core of who they are.

Too often young children, and especially teenagers, keep the deepest matters of their lives buried and hidden from their parents. They don't feel invited to share. Or perhaps they're just afraid of being ignored or rejected if they pour out their true feelings, needs, and concerns. But you as their parent are the very one God has commissioned to love them at this level.

That's why taking time to ask heart-to-heart questions and listening to your children are such vital components to your parenting. Your tender ear creates a safe and protected space for your child to bear their soul to you.

Since most conversations usually start at a surface level, children will often share childish and unimportant matters early on—what they saw on TV, what someone did at school, or their latest and greatest interests. If you ignore them or disregard their words in these shallow places, they may not feel safe to go any deeper with you. But if it's important to them, it should become important to you. By valuing them and assuring them of your interest and love, they will be more willing to share their deeper needs, feelings, and concerns with you.

Whether you are talking with them in the car, over the phone, or embracing them by their bedside, your job is to carefully cherish and love your children when they open up their hearts. They may be saying things that are completely off-base. They may be blinded or emotional. They may even need to be rebuked. But by first giving them your undivided attention and simply clarifying back what they said, they can at least know they've been heard. If they believe that you understand and care, they will trust you more completely and better value your counsel or concerns.

In contrast, bitter and rebellious teenagers often feel like their parents do not take time to listen or understand them. Since "good understanding produces favor" (Proverbs 13:15), all parents should frequently initiate safe conversations with their children to keep everyone's hearts closely tied together. Yes, the energy and time required in listening is a *sacrifice* of love, but the prospect of having your child's heart turns it into a very profitable investment.

Sometimes our challenge is in drawing them out so we can discover what they're really thinking. In cases like these, listening can ironically require doing more talking and gentle probing. But love can give us the patience for that.

"It sounds like you've really been going through a lot."

"Let me be sure I'm hearing you right."

"I can see how that would make you feel uncomfortable."

Most of the time when love listens, it's not carrying on a crime investigation or a call-in hotline. Nor is it jumping ahead to a quick fix. It's just listening and loving. Sincerely caring and sharing understanding with someone.

Listening also prepares your children to one day develop an intimate walk with God in prayer. "Call upon Me and come and pray to Me," He says, "and I will listen to you" (Jeremiah 29:12). "If any of you lacks wisdom, he should ask God, who gives to all generously and without criticizing, and it will be given to him" (James 1:5 HCSB).

Jesus built His own argument for prayer on how parents lovingly respond to their children's needs. "What man is there among you who, when his son asks for a loaf, will give him a stone? Or if he asks for a fish, he will not give him a snake, will he? How much more will your Father who is in heaven give what is good to those who ask Him" (Matthew 7:9–11).

God is faithful to listen when we call. So when our children ask to talk, we won't give them a busy signal. *Will we?* Our children should daily live with that same confidence in our love.

TAKE EACH OF YOUR KIDS OUT SOON FOR
A SPECIAL MEAL ALONE WITH YOU. PLAN ON
SPENDING MOST OF THE TIME JUST LISTENING.
ASK THEM QUESTIONS ABOUT THEIR HOPES,
DREAMS, CONCERNS, AND GOALS. REMEMBER
TO HELP THEM FEEL SAFE AS YOU PURSUE
A SENSE OF MUTUAL UNDERSTANDING.
AIM FOR THEIR HEART.

___ Check here when you've completed today's dare.

Where did you take them and what did you learn? How
awkward or enjoyable was the experience? What does this say
about the closeness of your relationship? What else can you do
to make it stronger?

_____

_____

_____

_____

_____

_____

*For help with today's dare, see "Questions to Ask Your Child"
on page 221 in the appendix.*

Certainly God has heard; He has given heed to the voice of my prayer. (Psalm 66:19)

DAY 30
Love shepherds hearts

He protects His flock like a shepherd; He gathers the lambs in His arms and carries them in the fold of His garment. (Isaiah 40:11 HCSB)

What does love do when something bad happens?

Life is sadly full of disappointments. We could wish it was all swing sets and snowmen and summers by the swimming pool. But children can sometimes come down with unexpected sicknesses. They can be knocked out of a sports season by a freak injury. Their aunt and uncle can get a divorce.

What does love do then? When grandmothers die. When their best friend betrays their trust. When they're not picked in a tryout. When someone from the opposite sex breaks their heart. How does love respond?

Being a good parent can often mean shifting our children to new expectations, thinking ahead of them when they aren't thinking at all. Love is intent on making sure we're tending to their hearts, not just their hurts. Making sure these unwelcome changes on the outside can be used by God to strengthen them on the inside, preparing them for lives of resiliency and grace.

The biblical model of strong leadership is that of a loving shepherd. It's one of constant provision and oversight, managing the day-to-day mechanics of the flock's physical needs. It's a task of both tender care and heroic rescue, noticing quickly when the sheep are under duress, frequently scanning the perimeters for predator attacks.

As shepherds in our homes, parents perform the functions of keeping bread on the table and clean socks in the top drawer. But much more important, we guard and shepherd our children's hearts. And at no time are their hearts more vulnerable—or more teachable—than when damaged or challenged by life's cruel, upsetting, and unwanted disappointments.

Loving parents stay on call for these emergencies. They keep themselves spiritually sharp and emotionally sensitive. Thinking ahead. Even when life is traveling along fairly smoothly, they want to be prepped for fresh infusions of God's wisdom when they may need it most. Instead of relying solely on emergency prayer, they ready themselves and their kids by better learning God's Word and God's heart. They stock up beforehand on provisions of biblical food and drink, and they keep them in ready storage to apply directly to any child's coming crisis.

So when we lose a loved one to accident, age, or sickness, love takes our kids directly into our arms and into the Word, where God promises to walk us "through the valley of the shadow of death" (Psalm 23:4). We remind them He is always with us and comforts us.

When our kids are wrongly accused or mistreated by a peer, a shepherding parent thinks ahead, knowing our child will be tempted toward revenge or subjected to feelings of self-doubt and insecurity. So we help them talk out and think through the best responses for each dynamic they are wrestling with—the confusion, the anger. We teach them the importance of prayer, as well as the release of forgiveness, helping to spare them the "torturers" of bitterness, outrage, and cold-heartedness (Matthew 18:34). Showing them how to lovingly confront if needed. Helping them be stronger as a result.

Love shows them how to deal with their fears by exposing lies, confronting shadows, and calling on the "strong tower" of the name of the Lord. "The righteous run to it," the Bible says, "and are protected" (Proverbs 18:10 HCSB).

Love shows them how to respond to failure, suffering, and disappointment, trusting that "God causes all things to work together for good to those who love God, to those who are called according to His purpose" (Romans 8:28).

Love even helps them learn to be content with not understanding how some things could ever happen in the first place. Unanswerable questions. As long as God knows and has already thought of everything they need, they can rest assured they will get through it. They can trust Him.

Sometimes love bundles them up in our tearful compassion. Other times, love must tell them to stand tall and shake it off, to head back into battle and let God's approval be their defense. "The LORD is for me; I will not fear; what can man do to me?" (Psalm 118:6)

This is parental shepherding.

This is how we guide and direct their hearts.

Fathers—the ones who are actually the most responsible for guarding, protecting, and preparing the hearts of their kids—are too often the first to withdraw when these challenging situations arise. They want to go back to their work, leave the sensitive stuff to their wives, or presume their children are strong enough to handle these issues without hands-on help. But we men must readily step up to the plate when needed. The Bible speaks often of what happens when sheep have no shepherd. They are scattered and left to wander. Sitting ducks, easily seduced into lies and error.

Our model is Jesus, the "good shepherd," who "lays down His life for the sheep" (John 10:11), in order that not a single one of them is snatched away or left to walk alone.

Yes, life is hard. But love is harder working. Stronger. Wiser. Able to keep our kids ready for anything, and responding to everything with grace and courage.

USING JOHN 16:32–33 AND ROMANS 8:28–39, DISCUSS WITH YOUR CHILDREN TODAY WHAT THEY SHOULD KEEP IN MIND AND HOW THEY SHOULD RESPOND WHEN HARD TIMES COME. IF THERE HAS BEEN A RECENT CRISIS, TALK IT THROUGH WITH THEM, ENCOURAGE THEM, AND PRAY FOR THEM.

___ Check here when you've completed today's dare.

What did you share with your children, and how did they receive it?

... that their hearts may be encouraged, having been knit together in love. (Colossians 2:2)

DAY 31
Love influences

Where there is no guidance the people fall,
but in abundance of counselors there is victory. (Proverbs 11:14)

Parenting was never intended to be a one-stop shop. As
solid as our personal knowledge may be, there will always be a
wide variety of notes we don't have the voice to sing.

This is why one of the boldest, most farsighted projects love
ever builds for our children is a strong network of influences
that can help us guide them down a trusted path in life.

It starts in our own homes, determining which windows we
want to open to the world and how best to utilize them for the
development of our children's minds and hearts.

One tool whose importance is often overlooked involves
directing our kids toward good books and literature. Reading
alone or together as a family from heroic Christian biographies
and classic masterpieces can fire their imaginations and inspire
them to emulate both real-life and fictional heroes. Grace.
Honor. Courage. Character. Igniting their thirst for discovery
and teaching them to love reading will be a lifelong investment
worth every minute and dollar spent.

Our musical choices, too, can cement in our children a taste
for real beauty and worship. Instead of leaving it up to their
friends to decide what kind of music they're supposed to like,
we as parents should keep our homes filled with joyful, edifying songs that point them to God and inspire them to trust
Him throughout their day. The entire book of Psalms is filled
with songs of praise passed down from generation to generation to help families worship and know God intimately.

Parents should also build a network of intercessory prayer support around their children throughout their lives. Who do you know who can join you in praying often for your kids?

In addition, they need the Bible and its principles to be taught and lived out on purpose before their eyes. We should read it to them and also teach them to study it on their own.

They need us to keep a careful eye on what passes for fun around the house so that evil is not masquerading as family entertainment, so that fantasy doesn't replace reality, and so that wasting time doesn't become their favorite activity. Good movies, positive Internet sites, and edifying activities need to replace the poisonous, vain, and foolish ones.

But beyond what happens inside the walls of our homes, we need trusted people who can help us do some of the heavy lifting and molding of hearts. Almost like a board of directors, we should empower other key individuals to speak into our children's lives and share the benefits of acquired wisdom.

For example, instead of just letting them see the pastor and other ministers from a distance on Sundays, invite different ones and their families into your home at various times—not merely to enjoy a meal, but to engage with your kids in rich conversations. Pull in other parents and grandparents who have been successful in raising their own kids, letting them speak into your son or daughter's life.

Guard who is teaching your children at church or at school. Get to know them and pray for them—that they would use their influence for good and for instilling faith, morality, and solid teaching into the next generation.

If your children are gravitating toward a certain field of interest, look for people who are professionally skilled in that capacity. See if your child can meet them, visit their job site, or maybe even gain a chance to try their hand at their craft.

Teach your children how to choose wise friends and avoid foolish ones. (Proverbs 13:20 and 1 Corinthians 15:33 are good verses to memorize with your kids along these lines.) Get to know your child's peers and their families. Have them over. Listen to their conversations, discern where they are, and lead the discussions and activities in a healthy direction. Train each of your children to discern wisely, stand alone, and willingly replace the demons with the angels.

Granted, there's a conspiracy to this. Your kids may not even realize how deliberately you're working to encircle them with godly voices, solid teaching, and powerful inspiration. But regardless, you'll see how much more your love can accomplish by uniting your efforts with a variety of wise co-conspirators.

Think of it as placing your child in a river of influence. Rivers, we know, come from many small streams that join up at critical junctures and unite into a rush of flow and direction. By virtue of your love, your children can sail downstream on that kind of river, carried along by the shared experiences, great coaches, and mighty mentors you have placed in their lives.

"How blessed," the Bible says, "is the man who does not walk in the counsel of the wicked, nor stand in the path of sinners, nor sit in the seat of scoffers" (Psalm 1:1). But what if instead of merely training your children to avoid these kinds of negative influences, you chartered them a life voyage with the virtuous, upright, and admirable, letting them stand with men and women of courage and godly integrity, offering them opportunities to sit down with people of wisdom and purpose?

A game plan like this will go a long way toward ensuring your family won't be "overcome by evil," but rather will "overcome evil with good" (Romans 12:21).

MAKE A LIST OF SOLID CHRISTIAN BOOKS, MUSICAL ARTISTS, AND INSPIRATIONAL MOVIES THAT YOU WANT TO PURCHASE FOR YOUR CHILDREN OVER THE NEXT YEAR, WORKING TO BUILD UP A LIBRARY OF INFLUENCE TO HELP THEM GROW IN WISDOM AND KNOWLEDGE. PURCHASE ONE OR MORE OF THESE ITEMS THIS WEEK AND GIVE IT TO YOUR CHILDREN AS A GIFT.

___ Check here when you've completed today's dare.

What came to mind as possibilities for building their "library"? How do you intend to use these items to their full potential?

He who walks with wise men will be wise,
but the companion of fools will suffer harm. (Proverbs 13:20)

DAY 32
Love prepares

The plans of the diligent lead surely to advantage. (Proverbs 21:5)

Love often calls upon us to act at a moment's notice. Problems arise. Conflict erupts. The day's events take an unexpected turn. And so we improvise on the fly. We see our children having a crisis, and we quickly respond to resolve it.

But love is also prudent. It thinks ahead and minimizes potential fallout by making strategic preparations. Love doesn't wait for the fires of life to consume our families; it installs smoke detectors and sprinkler heads beforehand.

Many of the problems your children will face aren't yet screaming for their attention. But one day they will. And when they do, your kids need to find that your love has equipped them ahead of time, by strapping on their parachutes early instead of plunging headlong out of the plane after them, hoping you aren't too late.

We want our children ready for life, not merely reacting to it. Expectant, not uninformed. Confident, not confused. Knowing which path to take, not guessing. So look for opportunities before each new season and major transition in their lives when you can sit down and explain what's coming up, shedding light on any current mysteries in their young minds.

Some of your preparations should orbit around significant occasions in your family life. A funeral, for instance, can trouble a young child. People are crying. The casket. The body. The graveyard. These may likely be the first real-life images your children have ever seen of death and mourning, dealing with the loss of someone close to them.

But it's also a distinct opportunity, in the days and hours beforehand, to open up the Scriptures with them. To explain why death is part of life. To point out what Jesus has already done to overcome death for all those who entrust themselves to Him. To tell them before the funeral what's about to happen and how they should respond. Rather than letting our children be shocked and forced to grapple with confusing thoughts and unwanted memories, love sets their hearts and minds on ready.

A wedding also, with its candlelit traditions, the rented clothes, and the eager kiss, gives you a similar, much happier occasion to talk with your kids about what they will see, how they should celebrate, and why marriage is God's design for romantic love and new families.

Other such moments involve traditional rites of passage. Twelve years of age, for example, should bring on a parental celebration and introduction into young adulthood. *Here's what is happening to your body, and here's how to survive your teen years.*

As sixteen approaches, we should equip them for new driving responsibilities and handling expanded freedoms. More than a themed birthday party or dinner at their favorite restaurant, these are monumental moments to celebrate. Love won't let them slip by without planning a special evening or weekend to devote some one-on-one time to discuss, encourage, and help them prepare for the upcoming years.

Intertwined among these milestones are other obligations for preparing our children well: puberty, their first job, graduation, leaving home, getting married. Parents tend to run from certain topics. But love is only concerned with the future well-being of our kids, knowing they need someone to equip them with everything required for making sound decisions, moral commitments, and healthy, Christ-centered approaches to the temptations, opportunities, and challenges they will face.

Discussions about purity and God's design for sex can be daunting for some. But ideally, love fosters an environment early enough where sensitive matters are dealt with in honest, tender, low-pressure contexts. You don't want their peers or the world indoctrinating them instead of you. Discussions about their bodies, their hearts, and the types of pressures to anticipate from the opposite gender will need to be on your radar.

But even if you're jump-starting conversations that should have happened already, let love lead you courageously now into matters too important to be left to chance or hearsay.

Love owes our kids the gift of truth. The gift of gleaning from our own history and observations rather than being left to drive in the dark and hope for the best. The gift of seeing how wisdom and God's Word will always outline a much better, trusted path toward self-respect and true love.

These conversations are not one-time encounters with our kids, never to be spoken of again, pretending like they didn't happen. They should grow and develop. Your child may be way too young right now to be burdened with some topics. They may pose questions you need to think long and hard about before answering. But whether you're dealing with training wheels, courtship parameters, or money management issues, the goal is not to check something off your list but to keep writing key principles across their hearts, year after year. You're preparing them for life. For success in every direction.

Being a parent brings plenty of carefree moments with our kids. Game nights. Saturdays. Summertime. And while your children will hopefully look back and remember the fun you had, your love can make sure they're also able to look ahead, prepared by what you sat down to carefully explain. Be a parent who didn't ignore the flying arrows, but who helped your children pick up their sword and shield.

TODAY'S DARE

MAKE A LIST OF IMPORTANT TOPICS YOU NEED
TO DISCUSS WITH YOUR CHILDREN: RELATION-
SHIPS, PUBERTY, INTEGRITY, FINANCES, ETC.
BEGIN NOW PLANNING ON THE RIGHT TIMES
TO HAVE THESE CONVERSATIONS. THEN START
DOING YOUR HOMEWORK IN PREPARATION
FOR THOSE DAYS. FINALLY, SPEND TIME
PRAYING FOR WISDOM AND GUIDANCE.

___ Check here when you've completed today's dare.

What conversations are your children ready for now? Which
ones need to wait a while, but not be forgotten?

_____

_____

_____

_____

_____

_____

_____

_____

_____

_____

_____

_____

*Build up, build up, prepare the way, remove every
obstacle out of the way of My people. (Isaiah 57:14)*

DAY 33
Love blesses

The LORD bless you, and keep you; the LORD make His face
shine on you, and be gracious to you. (Numbers 6:24–25)

One of the great joys of parenting is the opportunity to
know and *love* another person from the moment of their birth.
To watch them discover the world with wonder. To see them
grow physically and relationally. Day after day. Season after
season. Firsthand and front row.

Enjoying the journey of seeing them . . . become.

But a hidden key to children truly becoming the persons
God created them to be involves a parent's influence in that
direction—not by manipulation or force but by the intentional watering of the seeds God has planted. By giving them
a *blessing.*

But what exactly *is* a blessing?

Consider this contrast. No parent hopes their child grows
up to be a failure. Our love wants nothing but health, happiness, and God's best for each of them. A blessing is simply a
God-ordained way to handle these loving desires for our children, turning them from hopeful wishes into future realities.

To bless someone actually means "to speak well of." It's a
parent using their God-given authority to verbally affirm their
children for who they are, while also encouraging and inspir-
ing them towards future success.

In a blessing, powerful words and wishes combine with
prayers and praise. God instructed Moses to teach the high
priests how to bless the sons of Israel. "Say to them: 'The LORD
bless you, and keep you; the LORD make His face shine on you,
and be gracious to you; the LORD lift up His countenance on

you, and give you peace.' So they shall invoke My name on the sons of Israel, and I then will bless them" (Numbers 6:24–27).

As heavenly Father, God set up a pattern of blessing for His people: verbally affirming His acceptance and support of them, painting vivid pictures of their expected future, and investing Himself and His resources to make His words a reality.

The Bible is filled with dynamic blessings. From the beginning of recorded time, God "blessed" the first man and woman with the responsibility of being fruitful and multiplying (Genesis 1:28). He blessed Abraham, Isaac, and Jacob, who in turn blessed their children after them. Jacob uniquely blessed each of his twelve sons "with the blessing appropriate to him" (Genesis 49:28). Often in Scripture, people would place their hands on little children or take them lovingly into their arms to bless them (Genesis 48:14; Luke 2:28; Mark 10:16).

Through blessings, God continually inspired His people toward lives not only of usefulness, faith, and service, but also of hope, peace, and honor. His blessing urged them forward, renewed their confidence, and prepared the ground beneath their feet. It strategically launched them on a path of purpose toward spiritual prosperity.

After Jesus was baptized, a voice came from heaven: "You are My beloved Son, in You I am well-pleased" (Mark 1:11). God the Father publicly affirmed and blessed His Son, and then invested in Jesus' future success by immediately sending His Holy Spirit to fill Him (Luke 3:22). This powerful experience set Jesus up to completely fulfill the will of His heavenly Father during His earthly ministry.

Many children, even grown adults, long for but rarely if ever hear statements of love and approval from their parents. By simply saying, "You are my son (my daughter) and I dearly love you; I am so pleased with you and hope and pray God's very best for your life," you can change their lives forever. You can build the ideal setting for future wings to take flight.

Pointing out a child's skills or character could be part of a blessing. Say things like:

"I could see you becoming a great . . ."

"With your strengths and abilities, you could probably . . ."

"What impresses me is your giftedness and heart for . . ."

Then follow these words of blessing by your investment. Prayer. Encouragement. Introducing them to individuals of influence in that area. Giving them opportunities and the things they will need to help them succeed. This is not about pre-determining a college major or planning their career path. God will lead them through those matters in His time. But your ongoing encouragement will keep fresh wind in their sails as they navigate which paths to take.

Your blessing can enable them to see themselves as a chosen part of God's plan and His work on Earth within their generation. It can remind them of the grander reasons why He has endowed them with such talent, surrounded them with specific opportunities, and made them "His workmanship, created in Christ Jesus for good works, which God prepared beforehand" (Ephesians 2:10).

As your blessing soaks into their hearts, they can progress without feeling the need to find outside approval from unhealthy sources. They will stop living insecurely and start living confidently, free from fear and self-doubt.

When God blesses us, He is forecasting His favor, guiding us toward abundant life. So don't be afraid to speak your own words of blessing over your children. Don't fail to cast a vision that spurs them on to consider what wonderful things God could accomplish through them. The lives they could touch. The difference they could make. The blessing they could be.

TODAY'S DARE

WRITE OUT A SPECIAL BLESSING FOR
EACH OF YOUR CHILDREN, INCORPORATING
WHAT YOU SEE IN THEM AND WHAT YOU
ENCOURAGE THEM TO PURSUE AS GOD
GUIDES AND PROVIDES. READ IT OR SPEAK IT
ALOUD TO THEM AS A FAMILY. PRAY OVER
THEM THAT GOD WOULD BRING HIS PERFECT
PLANS TO PASS IN THEIR LIVES.

___ Check here when you've completed today's dare.

How did your children respond to your blessing? How could
you keep reinforcing your observations, leading your kids
toward the full experience of who they are?

_____

_____

_____

_____

_____

_____

_____

Bring them to me, please, that I may bless them. (Genesis 48:9)

DAY 34
Love and marriage

He who finds a wife finds a good thing
and obtains favor from the LORD. (Proverbs 18:22)

Most likely, if your children are still at home, the thought
of their getting married doesn't invade your mind very often.
But regardless of their age, it is never too early to begin training their minds and prioritizing your prayers to encompass
their future families. Near the top of your list should be regular
requests for God to preserve and prepare your child to one day
become and find a wonderful, godly spouse.

We all know how paramount a person's marital decisions
can be. How this one relationship will uniquely impact their
entire trajectory in life. It can unfold into years of peace, joy,
and celebration, or decades of suffering and limitation.

For better or worse.

That's basically how Deuteronomy 7 describes it. After
commanding His people to train their children well, God
warned Israel not to intermarry their sons and daughters with
the idolatrous nations around them. He knew that faithless
and foolish spouses could destroy the purity and derail the
legacy of many godly generations. So He warned His people
to be faithful to this important commandment, that they and
their children would continue enjoying the blessings of His
covenant love: His prosperity in their homes and families, His
protection against hunger and danger, His unmatched contentment in their pure and holy lives. If they ignored Him, their
families would eventually perish—one home, one dream, one
destructive consequence at a time.

The passing centuries have only reinforced this truth. King Solomon was the wisest man alive during his day, but his failure to guard carefully who he married was the very thing that ultimately defiled his faith and dethroned his family from further ruling the kingdom (1 Kings 11:1–13).

As he and many others have discovered, an innate friction arises when believers are "unequally yoked" with unbelievers (2 Corinthians 6:14 KJV). They have opposing masters and are heading in opposite directions. So if we do not guard against this dynamic and help our children marry vibrant, growing Christians, it could steal away their hearts and their futures.

In every marriage, the faith and unity of future generations hangs in the balance. So this is where a parent's love steps in. Ahead of time.

Looking down the road toward your child's marriage involves, first, *strategic prayer*. Start praying now for your sons to grow up, pursue, and marry Proverbs 31 women, and for your daughters to attract and marry Psalm 112 men. Train them to look beyond charm and outward attractiveness and seek spouses who have pure, wise, and honest hearts that love and fear God and are loyal to Him above all else (Proverbs 31:30).

In addition to this, preparing our kids' hearts for holy matrimony entails something else: *guarding the holiness of their purity*. Both by instruction and by example.

Young lust and sexual promiscuity do not lead to strong and faithful marriages. Instead, they dishonor and fracture them before they start (1 Thessalonians 4:1–7). We must teach our sons and daughters that true love is patient, pursues God's best, and protects the honor of others as well as the future marriage bed (Hebrews 13:4). Any moral compromise will store up guilt and shame in your child while attracting more of the wrong people, not to mention displeasing God.

Seasons will come when strong feelings will swirl. And love will call us to champion our kids' commitment to patience and purity by leading them to Scripture (2 Timothy 2:22), refocusing them on serving God without distraction (1 Corinthians 7:32–35), and helping them guard their bodies and hearts for God's best (1 Corinthians 6:9–20; Proverbs 4:23).

But that's not all. Our personal examples must set the tone. Are we loving and respectful toward each other as husband and wife—forgiving, patient, and kind? Are we showing our kids how to love a woman, how to respect a man, and how to treat the opposite sex by the way we cherish one another?

One of love's high-level jobs is to show our children that while no marriage is perfect, all marriages can be loving. Including ours. Even if you're a single or divorced parent, you can look for ways to live out and encourage the biblical standards of love, purity, and faithfulness you desire for them.

For after our children marry, our obligations will shift from hands-on discipleship to hands-off respect for their new family and independence. We can encourage, pray, and offer our counsel when asked. But we'll need to give them space to "leave and cleave" so their new, "one flesh" union can bloom. Meddling or rescuing will only hold them back, planting a weed of division between them and a root of resentment toward you.

Until they are ready, however, the Scripture repeatedly urges young people not to "stir up or awaken love until the appropriate time" (Song of Solomon 2:7; 3:5; 8:4 HCSB).

Praying and preserving our children's innocence and honor, protecting what we expose them to, and discouraging premature boyfriend/girlfriend relationships before they are near marrying age—these are loving, careful steps that parents should take to help young hearts stay pure and to set up our children for long-term success at the altar.

SHARE WITH YOUR CHILDREN THE IMPOR-
TANCE OF MARRYING THE RIGHT PERSON.
PRAY SPECIFICALLY TODAY FOR THEIR FUTURE
SPOUSES, THAT GOD WOULD BE PRESERVING
THEM IN PURITY AND MATURING THEM IN
CHRISTIAN FAITH. IF YOUR CHILDREN ARE
ALREADY MARRIED, PRAY THAT THEIR
MARRIAGES WOULD BE STEADFAST,
INTIMATE, AND LOVING.

__ Check here when you've completed today's dare.

How did your children receive your encouragement? What
other kinds of qualities in your future sons- and daughters-in-
law is God leading you to pray for?

Encourage the young women to love their husbands. . . .
Encourage the young men to be sensible about everything. (Titus 2:4, 6 HCSB)

Love rejoices in truth

He who is steadfast in righteousness
will attain to life. (Proverbs 11:19)

Few things should excite our hearts more completely than when we see our kids loving God and living with godly virtue. Proving to be a true, caring friend. Respecting authority. Practicing modesty. Carrying themselves with maturity, wisdom, and kindness.

When our children exhibit attitudes and behaviors that fall in line with what God desires from them, they shouldn't be left to guess how much it pleases us. When they are actually living out the truths of Scripture—when we see them being unselfish, sacrificial, and servant-hearted—they need to know we will not let it go unnoticed. We will celebrate it.

The apostle John said, "I have no greater joy than this, to hear of my children walking in the truth" (3 John 4). He rejoiced when his spiritual children were pursuing godliness, purity, and faithfulness, remaining unjaded and uncompromising. He knew this was the only way they could please God, complete their purpose, and find true joy and fulfillment in life. So nothing pleased him more than seeing them practicing the priorities that kept them squarely in the path of blessing. Growing. Thriving.

Love "rejoices with the truth" (1 Corinthians 13:6). When your children are growing in Christian character, persevering in faith, and embracing roles of giving and service, the Bible says you should celebrate it. More than when they get a blue ribbon on field day. More than when they achieve success in their school or in their jobs.

The apostle Paul often expressed delight in his letters to the churches after hearing reports of their faithfulness and growth in Jesus (2 Thessalonians 1:3–4). As parents, we should be no less excited and eager to call out our own children's character for this kind of special recognition.

What makes you the most proud and overjoyed in your child? Is it when he hits a home run? When she gets an A in English class? Or are you more impressed when your son prays and reads his Bible in the morning, or when your daughter shares her faith or forgives her sister?

You are one of the most influential people in your child's life. They will want to please whoever praises them most. Have you been using your influence to lead them to honor God?

Take one spin through the TV channels or walk through any shopping mall, and you'll find out very quickly what the people in our society love and value—what they "rejoice" in. Vanity. Materialism. Sensuality. Self-centeredness.

It's as though the general population is walking around with a script in hand. With roles we're all expected to play. We've been told what we're supposed to think about and dress like, what we're supposed to find interesting and aspire to, what we're supposed to spend our money on and time doing. And if anyone decides to go off-message, they are likely to be ridiculed or rejected. Isolated. Ignored.

We must never forget that by encouraging our children to walk with God, we are asking them to intentionally travel against the cultural tide. In a world where externals rule the night and inner character gets little sunshine, their purity and loyalty to truth will likely label them as outdated and irrelevant. So if our kids choose to honor God with their lives and follow what we've taught them, they will earn request from some, but will be misunderstood and mocked by others.

This is why our love must always affirm the courageous strides they make in faithfulness, goodness, and self-sacrifice. Their commitment to the challenge of Scripture—"Do not be conformed to this world, but be transformed by the renewing of your mind" (Romans 12:2)—becomes much more attainable when strengthened by our backing and example.

With the love of the Father and the love of their parents behind them, they can know with profound assurance, "Blessed are you when men hate you, and ostracize you, and insult you, and scorn your name as evil, for the sake of the Son of Man. Be glad in that day and leap for joy, for behold, your reward is great in heaven" (Luke 6:22–23). If buoyed by your support and enthusiasm, they will more readily turn away from the temporary and shortsighted things in life, turning instead toward the eternal and spiritual (Colossians 3:1–2).

They need to be able to count on us as their greatest cheering section. They need parents who lift their heads and praise them for choosing to "detest evil" and "cling to what is good" (Romans 12:9 HCSB). We should be raising kids who know how to hate their sin while loving their God, who can tell when things are wrong—both in themselves and in the culture—and who still courageously "seek first the kingdom of God and His righteousness" (Matthew 6:33 HCSB).

Love your children enough, through both your parental counsel and your own personal delights, that they learn to love the blessings of obedience and truth. Train them to set their hearts and hopes on pleasing the "Audience of One" in heaven, regardless of what the rest of the world may expect of them.

And when you see them faithfully putting His Word into practice—*rejoice!*—loud and long enough for their spirits to celebrate with you. You'll be joining your own applause with the applause of heaven.

TODAY'S DARE

IDENTIFY A GODLY TRAIT YOU SEE IN
YOUR CHILDREN—A FAITHFUL WORK ETHIC,
A LOVE OF WORSHIP, A SELFLESS HEART—AND
THEN TRY LOCATING A SCRIPTURE VERSE THAT
ENCOURAGES THIS ATTITUDE OR ACTION. GIVE
SPECIAL NOTICE TO THEM WHILE EVERYONE IS
TOGETHER AS A FAMILY. READ OR QUOTE THE
VERSE YOU FOUND, AND TELL THEM WHY
IT REMINDS YOU OF THEM.

___ Check here when you've completed today's dare.

What attributes did you note about your children? How did
you affirm them?

_____

_____

_____

_____

_____

_____

Some verses to consider for today's dare:
Galatians 5:22–23; Philippians 2:3–5; Colossians 3:12–14

May the Lord direct your hearts into the love of God. (2 Thessalonians 3:5)

DAY 36
Love bears all things

You saw how the LORD *your God carried you, just as a man carries
his son, in all the way which you have walked.* (Deuteronomy 1:31)

Look back on your own youthful adventures—perhaps
at some of the very same ages of your children today—and
you can likely remember specific times when you failed to
be loving, kind, and readily responsible. You failed to honor
commitments or always keep a level head. From the acci-
dental to the stubborn and intentional, we all did things that
were clearly wrong. And in one way or another, we eventually
paid a price.

The Bible says it this way: "Do not be deceived, God is
not mocked; for whatever a man sows, this he will also reap"
(Galatians 6:7).

But think back: was the love of your parents one of the
costs you paid? You may have thought so, especially if your
misbehavior spiraled into full-blown rebellion. You may have
consistently exhausted your parents' patience, and they grew
very weary of putting up with you. Whether true or not, the
real question is how you will respond if or when *your* children
fail. Love, the Bible says, "bears all things" (1 Corinthians 13:7).
It endures. Even if the choices made by your kids cause you
deep pain and disappointment.

The Devil will make sure our children always live with the
option of choosing the wrong path. Like us, they will grapple
with weaknesses in their humanity. They will be susceptible at
times to subtle deception. They may struggle to surrender their
hearts and decisions to God, not always understanding that His
Word is giving them the whole story.

That's when we as parents find out if our love for them is only as deep as the laughter we shared during the good times, or if it's all-encompassing enough to stay with them in their hardheartedness and brokenness. Will we angrily focus on what their misbehavior is costing *us*? Or will our love spring up to seek their restoration and rescue? To bear with them in love?

Are your children allowed to fail at all? Can they be imperfect in your world? Can they lose their way without losing the certainty of your love, steadfastness, and forgiveness?

Parents can greatly influence and impact their children, but they cannot force them to always choose the godly path. You may be the best parent in the world, but your son or daughter can still dive into seasons of rebellion.

Even God said of His chosen people, "I have raised children and brought them up, but they have rebelled against Me" (Isaiah 1:2 HCSB). He later warned them, "If you are willing and obedient, you will eat the good things of the land. But if you refuse and rebel, you will be devoured by the sword" (Isaiah 1:19–20 HCSB).

Some of the greatest lessons in your children's lives will come from times when they are tested and forced to swallow the bitter consequences of their actions. In these situations, it's not always best to quickly rescue them from the wages of their own sin. You may actually be fighting against the Lord just as His Fatherly hand of discipline is striking a strategic blow (Hebrews 12:5–6). Too often parents foolishly step in and take the lick themselves, unknowingly hijacking the lesson God is delivering to their children.

So when does a parent turn up the heat, and when do they show compassion and mercy?

The Bible says, "God resists the proud, but gives grace to the humble" (James 4:6 HCSB). Humility—this is the key.

When Jesus was describing the heart of our heavenly Father, He told the powerful story of a prodigal son who pridefully demanded his inheritance early, squandered his father's wealth, and ended up penniless, eating with the pigs.

His father did not rescue him. Not in his pride. But when the son came to his senses, he humbly went home. And "while he was still a long way off, his father saw him and felt compassion for him, and ran and embraced him and kissed him."

Instead of immediately lecturing him, the father recognized humble brokenness in his son, and said, "Quickly bring out the best robe and put it on him. . . . Let us eat and celebrate; for this son of mine was dead and has come to life again; he was lost and has been found" (Luke 15:22–24).

Jesus used this amazing story to describe the grace-filled heart of our heavenly Father. And it should be our heart as well.

God repeatedly reached out to His chosen, again and again—not in weak permissiveness, but in steadfast love. By His grace, He covered their shame and multiplied His mercies. They always had a home to come back to. Their home was Him.

Love says, "I'm not going to bail you out of jail, but I will visit you when you are there and joyfully receive you in my arms when you come to your senses and come home."

Rebellious children can break the hearts of their parents. They can cause deep anger and confusion. But ultimately, your love can continue to "bear all things" for them. Not to get bitter in your brokenness, but to keep speaking the truth in tough love and giving them back to the Lord, again and again. To rally an army of intercessors. To pray down heaven and earth on their behalf. You may need to ask for God's measured discipline first before His divine rescue and mercy. But when they wake up and turn back, your love needs to be standing at the door with arms open wide.

IF ONE OF YOUR CHILDREN IS IN
A PERIOD OF TURMOIL AND CONFUSION,
WRITE A SHORT NOTE TO ASSURE THEM OF
YOUR CONSISTENT LOVE, PRAYER, AND SUP-
PORT. MAKE A POINT TO TELL EACH OF YOUR
KIDS THAT YOUR LOVE IS A CONSTANT, NO
MATTER WHAT. ASK IF THERE'S SOMETHING
YOU CAN HELP BEAR FOR THEM TODAY.

___ Check here when you've completed today's dare.

What is challenging your love the most in your children right
now? What is love calling you to do that you haven't done
before?

He put up with them in the wilderness. (Acts 13:18)

DAY 37
Love fulfills dreams

I will most gladly spend and be
expended for your souls. (2 Corinthians 12:15)

God loves with extravagance. He enjoys going way over and above. He pours out freely beyond measure. The Bible says He "lavished" His grace on us (Ephesians 1:8), that He provides us abundant life overflowing beyond limitations (John 10:10).

And we as His disciples are called to give that same kind of extravagant love—to give more than is asked of us, to go the extra mile, to exceed what is expected (Matthew 5:39–45). The Scripture tells us that God delights in cheerful, hilarious givers (2 Corinthians 9:7), those who are willing to give in abundance out of joyful delight.

Think right now of each of your kids. What is something they would really, really love to have or do? What would they deeply long to experience or learn? Who would they love to meet? What would cause them to say, "This is the best day ever!"?

Parenting doesn't always have to mean coming up with another creative reason *not* to do something. Imagine what might happen if the one thing your son or daughter would never expect or think you'd ever do for them became the next big thing you did?

What unexpected gift could you start saving up for that would overwhelm your child with love? A bicycle? A trampoline? A puppy? A car? Where could you arrange to take them for an unexpected family adventure? An amusement park? A camping trip? A hot air balloon ride?

Love sometimes needs to be extravagant. To go all out. To figure out the technicalities, open up the floodgates of generosity, and bless someone unexpectedly out of sheer joy. Common sense tells us we can't give them everything they might like. Our budgets and schedules are limited as it is. But not everything your child wants has a hefty price tag. Joy comes in all sorts of shapes and sizes.

You may have a preschooler whose idea of the perfect day is simply a kid's meal for lunch and then playing with you on the playground afterward. Your teenage son may just want you to throw the football with him in the backyard. Your daughter's heart might burst if you merely cleaned her closet or took her to a nice restaurant in your Sunday best. What is realistically within your grasp to make happen?

And what about some longer-term investments?

Inside your child's heart are lifelong dreams and desires placed there by Almighty God. Bigger hopes and passions that will one day draw out the full measure of their unique gifts and aspirations. Perhaps your kids don't dwell on them every day, but when they do, their hearts soar with hope. *What if . . . I wonder . . . I would love . . . One day . . .* They've likely shown an appetite for these things as long as you can remember. And as they age, these interests have likely narrowed into tighter fields of exploration. They spend time studying it. They want to get better at it. They can't help but talk about it.

You almost certainly could identify one or more passions that visibly ignite excitement in their eyes and voice. Learning to hunt. Playing a new sport or musical instrument. Going on a missions trip. Making movies one day.

We've all seen some extremes: parents who send off their children at nine years of age to pursue training as an Olympic athlete; parents who load up their children's summers with endless camps and competitions to help develop their skills and repertoires. And while not every parent can or should go to these levels, love does inspire us not to squander our children's dreams or let them die a slow death from lack of parental support. Love measures our investment against whatever else consumes our time and attention, and determines to do what we feasibly can to foster what God has begun in them.

Jesus instructed His followers to "store up for yourselves treasures in heaven . . . for where your treasure is, there your heart will be also" (Matthew 6:19–21).

But what if you knew you had "treasures in heaven" right under your roof—boys and girls whose spirits will one day live forever with God . . . in heaven? Why would a lavish display of time, money, risk, and devotion, directed into them and their dreams, not be an investment with eternal implications?

Some would say this is spoiling them. And it *would* be if we allowed our children to selfishly make demands of us or act entitled. But we have a heavenly Father who by His own initiative freely gives to us (Romans 8:32), yet who wisely withholds those things He knows we shouldn't have. If our answer is "no" so often that we hardly consider the possibility of going beyond, we are not loving our kids with the love of our Father.

So dare to think in terms of overwhelming your children with love in some special way, to exceed all their expectations by your surprising thoughtfulness and kindness. Even if it's not something that sparks your own interests, consider the connection you could make with their heart by doing something extravagant.

Take note of your children's desires and dreams. Determine how you could reasonably help fulfill them or assist your child in accomplishing them. Then show them in living color what the extravagant love of their heavenly Father looks like.

BEGIN MAKING PLANS TO SPEND TIME OR
MONEY ON A SPECIAL GIFT OR EXPERIENCE
THAT WOULD OVERWHELM YOUR CHILD.
ENCOURAGE THEIR PASSION IN ONE OF THEIR
BIGGEST INTEREST AREAS. BE CREATIVE,
BE GENEROUS, AND BE COMMITTED
TO SEEING IT THROUGH.

___ Check here when you've completed today's dare.

What area comes to mind? How creative do you think you can
be with this surprise?

_____

_____

_____

_____

_____

_____

_____

_____

Children are not responsible to save up for their parents,
but parents for their children. (2 Corinthians 12:14)

DAY 38
Love liberates

I commit you to God and to the message of His grace. (Acts 20:32 HCSB)

"For this reason a man shall leave his father and his mother, and be joined to his wife; and they shall become one flesh" (Genesis 2:24).

This is the first time the words *mother* and *father* appear in Scripture. And surprisingly they don't merely describe a family together but a family separating—a son leaving the shelter of home to become married to his wife, where this same process will continue repeating itself, over and over, throughout the generations.

How quickly we reach this stage as parents, usually much sooner than we expect when it arrives. That normal feeling of having children at home—almost as if we can't remember it any other way—is gradually replaced by the inner, conflicted feeling of watching them leave us. All those years of daily love, preparation, and investment. The tricycles, the training wheels, the bicycles, the automobiles. And now the taillights.

Time passes like a vapor. A warm breath into the cold. And parents must willingly and courageously move on to the next season of their lives. No, we don't really want our kids young and dependent on us forever. And yet a big part of us surely will miss them when they're not.

The awareness that this transition is coming hangs over us as parents. It subtly slips into our conscious thoughts at every Christmas and birthday and each turn of the school year. It's always nearer than it was before. Always closer than we may be willing to admit or feel ready to handle emotionally.

In many ways, this is precisely what parenting is designed to do—to prepare our children for this day, when they will be out from under our control, responsible for themselves as young adults and readily lifting their wings to fly into the world and the future. Much of what we do as parents all along the way, when you think about it, is by design teaching our kids how to function independently of us and then leave.

So love must step up to this and not shy us away from our duty. It must keep us thinking ahead, forcing us to choose what's best in each season so our children will enjoy God's best overall. Love doesn't get so lost in the everyday grind and the weekly schedule that it fails to consider where all this activity should be taking us, where it's taking *our kids*. Love has good distance vision and doesn't wince to keep us from using it.

Little by little, especially as our kids begin cycling through the teen years, we need to be intentionally entrusting each of them with more and more appropriate, new levels of privilege and responsibility. Larger assignments. Harder jobs. Increasing amounts of freedom. Not before they possess the maturity and judgment to carry it, but we give it to them carefully, with a healthy balance of release.

Instead of doing everything *for* them, love chooses to let them learn what's involved in doing it themselves. Instead of holding back opportunities—even the ones they may be scared to take on—love lets them shoulder some risk, practiced inside environments that are safe enough for failure to be minimized and turned into life skill lessons. Eventually, there should be nothing they can't do without our help. They must be fully prepared to leave.

Jesus taught this principle in His parable of the talents, where a wise employer distributed individual amounts of money for each of His able servants to use and invest. He entrusted each of them with exactly as much as He knew they could handle. Then afterwards, those who had managed their delegated portions with care and sharpness, He freely rewarded them with even more, saying, "You were faithful with a few things, I will put you in charge of many things" (Matthew 25:21).

Jesus Himself, in His own ministry, was very deliberate about launching His disciples into their future. The gospel of John contains four full, red-letter chapters—nearly 20 percent of the entire book (chapters 14–17)—devoted entirely to instructing His closest followers about what was coming and how they could handle it after Jesus had left their side.

He gave them clear instructions and encouragement. He promised them His love and the Holy Spirit's ongoing presence. He assured them they were ready, that He had confidence in them. And He prayed with passionate zeal for their protection, their success, and their influence on the world.

Love gives us the distinct honor of investing in our children with this same kind of long-range view. We should make plain to them what is coming in the days ahead and what we're preparing them to do. We should promise to be there for them as they test their legs. We should give them benchmarks to shoot for, letting them know we're watching and cheering them on, ready to give them even more opportunities as they earn them. And then we pray like there's no tomorrow, knowing that what they truly need—more than their own sense of confidence and achievement, more than our parental backup—are ongoing experiences of trust with their heavenly Father, who will always be their Counselor and Guide.

Launching is hard. But this is our job. Prepare them well, and there's no limit to where your love can propel them.

CONSIDER AN ADDED RESPONSIBILITY
OR PRIVILEGE YOU COULD ENTRUST TO EACH
OF YOUR CHILDREN. CLEARLY OUTLINE THE
PARAMETERS, WHAT YOU EXPECT OF THEM,
AND WHAT THEIR FAITHFULNESS WILL MEAN.
IF YOUR CHILDREN ARE OLDER—PERHAPS
ALREADY OUT OF YOUR HOME—TRY CONTACT-
ING THEM TODAY AND REMINDING THEM OF
YOUR LOVE AND CONFIDENCE IN THEM,
YOUR PRIDE IN WHO THEY'RE BECOMING.

___ Check here when you've completed today's dare.

What responsibilities did you give them? How did they receive
them? What would help you keep doing this more often?

_____

_____

_____

_____

_____

_____

_____

_____

_____

_____

As You sent Me into the world, I also have sent them into the world. (John 17:18 HCSB)

DAY 39
Love never fails

I *have loved you with an everlasting love.* (Jeremiah 31:3)

Because of your role as a parent, you now understand love in a way you could have never understood it before. You've now held a child of your own in your arms. You've hugged and kissed away their hurts and fears. You've laughed at their unforgettable expressions and rushed over from across the backyard to save them from an accident waiting to happen. You've cleaned up after them, kept them supplied with shoes and clothes, always kept them fed, and brought them countless cups of water after praying over them at night.

Funny, you may have once felt very unsure that you even wanted children yet. Perhaps you didn't know if you were fully ready to have a son or daughter of your own. *Look how much you've changed. How deeply you love them now.*

But what if this same child ever turned away and rejected your love? What if they changed and pushed you away? What if they began to misread your loving intentions and accused you of being too heavy-handed, unrealistic, controlling? What if, in reacting to your weaknesses and mistakes, they chose to quit receiving your love at all—not believing or trusting you, not wanting you in their lives or their business? What if they were to drift so far away, you almost didn't recognize them anymore, completely losing your delight in what they have become?

What do you think *God* would do in circumstances like these? What has His love done in the past?

The word most often used in Scripture to describe God's covenant love is "loving-kindness." *Faithful* love. *Enduring* love. The kind that doesn't come with term limits or zoning restrictions. It transcends both time and space. Abundant. Established.

A permanent fixture.

The earth is so full of His loving-kindness (Psalm 33:5), it reaches all the way to the sky, climbing as high as the heavens (Psalm 36:5). His love is "everlasting" (1 Chronicles 16:34), like a song playing all day and all night (Psalm 42:8), then going on for the rest of our lives (Psalm 23:6). "Blessed be God, who has not turned away my prayer nor His lovingkindness from me" (Psalm 66:20). His love never fails.

Nor does it fail to bring comfort and confidence to the hearts of those to whom He directs His love. They may not always admit to needing it, or wanting it, or even believing it is there, but they are ever blessed by its presence nonetheless.

Is God still holy and set apart? Yes.

Powerful and to be feared?

Never to be taken lightly? Absolutely.

But God's love is still constant, always able to be trusted (Psalm 13:5). Unshakable, and therefore able to keep you from feeling shaken (Psalm 21:7). His love is a refuge under which you can always take cover (Psalm 36:7)—a stronghold, a song of strength (Psalm 59:16), able to make you flourish and grow and come back to life again (Psalm 52:8).

This is why we always run to Him instead of away from His holy eyes and judgment. His perfect love draws us in with trembling hearts to find peace and grace in His Fatherly arms.

Because of this, you can go to Him in your weakest, most impossible moments of parenting and find His strength able to help you continue to love your children. Even if they rebel or turn away, God's Spirit can give you what you no longer feel or could ever manufacture on your own. He can fill you with His unchanging and unending love (Romans 5:1–5). Loving your children relentlessly is more about staying close to Him than being pleased with *them*.

Even if your children stay pure and close to the Lord, they will still fail and find themselves struggling at various seasons. As long as you have breath, God wants you to be a source of stability and an example of His love to them in those hours.

Parenting is a long-term, lifetime deal. Notice how almost every verse and example of love cited in this chapter come from Old Testament Scripture—back in those pages of the Bible where some people only see God's anger and blazing judgment. Yet His love was still overwhelming and unfailing back then. And having now become flesh through the life of Jesus, having sacrificed Himself for our sin, and having defeated the curse of death over us through His cross, His love continues ever strong today and will never end for all eternity.

When God gave you children, He also gave you the opportunity to taste a little of what His love is like for His children. So when we look at God's love, we see the model for our own—love that's not based on the actions, temperament, or attitude of the one being loved, but rather on the one doing the loving.

Loving our children is a promise. A covenant. A chosen occupation. Times will change, and the needs of our kids will change with them. Life won't always give us the option of picking them up and holding them till they calm down and our love can get through. Sometimes our love must simply endure from a distance . . . to prove to them that it will always come out as love on the other side.

That's because love by nature is eternal. God's love is already what it will always be. It never ends. Never stops loving. And as you walk with Him, you can share that love with your children, because His "love never fails" (1 Corinthians 13:8).

TAKE A FEW MINUTES TO FOCUS ON GOD'S
LOVE FOR YOU. AS MUCH AS YOU LOVE YOUR
CHILDREN, HE LOVES BOTH THEM AND YOU
MUCH MORE. THANK HIM FOR HIS LOVE,
AND ASK HIM TO HELP YOU REFLECT IT
TO YOUR CHILDREN EACH DAY. TELL YOUR
CHILDREN THIS WEEK THAT YOU WILL LOVE
THEM NO MATTER WHAT THEY DO, WHERE
THEY GO, OR WHAT HAPPENS TO THEM—
BECAUSE THAT IS HOW GOD LOVES YOU,
AND THAT IS HOW YOU LOVE THEM.

___ Check here when you've completed today's dare.

Write out some of the ways God has shown His love to you and
your family.

Who is wise? Let him give heed to these things,
and consider the lovingkindnesses of the LORD. (Psalm 107:43)

DAY 40
Love leaves a legacy

"Your work will be rewarded," declares the LORD. *(Jeremiah 31:16* NIV)

There are no "perfect parents"—only good men and women who love their children to the very end. Through losing teeth, bumps and bruises, and countless sack lunches. Through midnight homework and sibling rivalry.

Sometimes it may feel as if we're just constantly caught in an endless cycle, trying to get through this season and keep it all from falling apart. But love is what helps us realize we've actually been building something great—a LEGACY.

A strong family heritage. An investment in countless generations that will follow us forward. That's what our love can help us envision when we close our eyes at night—the prospect of shaping future generations into warriors and winners and blessing them for years to come. We do this through daily sacrifice, hopeful dreaming, and heavy lifting.

But it all gets grounded in love, which is at the core of the legacy you will leave.

Its strength is not merely in the family name or the DNA you're passing on to your children. Your legacy of love will speak on, for example, through your *wisdom*.

Perhaps you don't think you have many priceless gems to be remembered. But most of those nuggets won't come from rehearsed lines or impressive speeches. They'll rather be mentioned offhand from the bedside, the dinner table, or the driver's seat. They will be caught as you whisper in your child's ears during a moment of crisis. Then your words will one day be repeated into the ears of your great-grandchildren. They won't know the source, but they will feel the impact. So by keeping your mind trained now on God's Word, learning to think His thoughts after Him, and letting His truth flow through your own experiences and memories, your children will embrace truth that is worth carrying on. It's part of your legacy.

Love will also last through your *example*. Whenever you're sorting out a household argument or dispute, you're not only trying to calm everybody down; you're showing your kids patience and perspective. When you're getting up early to pray and hear from God, you're instilling in them how faith orients a person's day. When you choose what seems right and best at this particular moment, you're anchoring morality into young minds. With everything you did wrong, your children will likely pass on what you did right. You're leaving a legacy.

Love will also continue forward through your *worship*. Your children will be allured by hundreds of things in life—money, popularity, entertainment. Each salesman, senator, and suitor will make his case for why he's worthy of your children's devotion. And though your kids will grow to make their own decisions, they will always be influenced by how *your* faith defined what really matters. How you loved and worshipped God. How you deferred to Him and His will. How you let His and not others' opinions form your identity.

This is part of your legacy. If not yet, it can be.

Over the years, you can always be an affirming voice in your children's hearts, giving them renewed confidence in the healthy, positive steps they're taking in life. You can be an open door of counsel, ever available with a ready ear and a wise word whenever they face decisions deeper than their understanding and experience. You may unexpectedly assist or bless them financially with a generous gift that lightens their load or cushions their crisis. You can pray, and pray, and never stop praying.

Then you can do all this all over again for your grandkids as opportunities arise and resources allow.

And it's all because of love—God's love—passed on daily through the love of a parent. Always there. Always in the back of their minds. Always with assurance, affection, and mercy. What starts with diapers and high chairs becomes a lifelong ministry and mission, investing your faith and yourself into one of the very few places where your impact can best affect generations.

Your body will age. Your clothes will become dated. Your place of employment will eventually move on to fresh replacements. Your various acquaintances will think of you occasionally, but only when something sparks their memory. Even your church will welcome new members and carry on its ministries without you. But the waves of your life and influence will continue to live on and ripple through the hearts, minds, and faith of your children. It's why one biblical writer prayed, "Even when I am old and gray, O God, do not forsake me, until I declare Your strength to this generation, Your power to all who are to come" (Psalm 71:18).

So be sure to pour the full weight of your love especially into this one place—in these precious, irreplaceable relationships—and you will bless God and the world through your children. Both now and for many years to come.

Ultimately, God gave you children so you could introduce them to Him and personally show them His love and His ways on Earth. We have written this book with the hope that one day in eternity, He will find you faithful to this sacred trust. Then He will introduce you to the many generations you blessed and helped lead into heaven. There we can see and enjoy His glory for all eternity.

This is the *Love Dare* for parents.

READ PSALM 71:18 AND WRITE OUT A LEGACY LETTER TO YOUR CHILDREN THAT THEY CAN PASS ON TO FUTURE GENERATIONS WHO WILL FOLLOW THEM. IN IT, SHARE A STATEMENT OF YOUR FAITH, YOUR VALUES, YOUR LOVE FOR THEM, AND YOUR HOPES FOR GOD'S RICHEST BLESSINGS ON THE FUTURE GENERATIONS YOU WILL ONE DAY LEAVE BEHIND. PRESENT THIS LETTER TO EACH OF YOUR CHILDREN (AND MAYBE GRANDCHILDREN) AS A GIFT AND LEGACY OF YOUR LIFE . . . AND YOUR LOVE.

___ Check here when you've completed today's dare.

How did you choose to give your children this legacy letter? What is your hope and prayer as you give it to them?

*Their descendants will serve Him; the next generation
will be told about the LORD. (Psalm 22:30 HCSB)*

Appendix Articles

APPENDIX I
What does the Bible say about spanking?

Discipline is a necessary and important part of loving parenting. Many parents wonder and ask if spanking is ever appropriate. While trends, customs, and opinions vary around the world, discipline remains a private matter between parents, their children, and God. The opinions of outsiders are not your authority and should not dictate what you do before God within your own family and home.

While some parents have sadly misused the practice of spanking to harmful extremes, we want to communicate clearly that no discipline should ever be destructive or result in emotional, spiritual, or physical abuse. However, the opposite is also true. A lack of discipline can be indirectly abusive and hateful towards children (Proverbs 13:24).

Balance is the key. For any form of discipline to be effective, children must respect it and take it seriously. Otherwise it becomes meaningless and your instructions will be ignored. While there are times when a stern lecture, grounding, extra work, or the removal of a privilege is the best course of action, the Scriptures clearly indicate that parents should not be afraid to lovingly spank their children when needed.

In Hebrews 12:5–11, the Bible explains the good purposes of discipline and states that God, our heavenly Father, lovingly chastens (spanks) all of His children even as an earthly father does. King Solomon noted, "Foolishness is bound up in the heart of a child; the rod of correction will drive it far from him" (Proverbs 22:15 NKJV). Proverbs 23:14 says, "Punish him with the rod and save his soul from death" (NIV).

In the Bible, the word "rod" actually means a small branch, stick, or reed-like item, not a large, dangerous weapon used for permanent bodily injury. Parents should never strike their children in the face or head, and never with a closed fist on *any* part of their body—which would amount to child abuse. A spanking is appropriately applied to the rear end, causing enough of a short sting to get the job done (dissuading future misbehavior and reinforcing your authority), but never to wound or scar a child physically or emotionally.

Many forms of discipline merely drag out and water down punishment, succeeding only in building anger and resentment in a child, whereas a parental spanking can be quickly applied, very effective, and over in seconds. "He who spares his rod hates his son, but he who loves him disciplines him promptly" (Proverbs 13:24 NKJV).

Still, some people frown upon any form of spanking. However, God's Word communicates that a child is better off experiencing a brief, physical sting for a few seconds than to grow up rebelling against their authorities and ignoring the consequences of their actions. What prisoner would not gladly exchange his current incarceration as an adult for a quick spanking as a child?

A loving spanking will not harm or warp a child; rather, it can humble and train them toward wisdom and maturity. It can thwart rebellion and yield greater respect for you and other authorities in the future. It can even increase the intimacy and closeness between parent and child.

The type and amount of any discipline should depend upon the child's age, understanding, attitude, and actions. Any discipline should be carefully applied with explanation, and followed by tender comfort, counsel, and affirmation. Parents should never discipline with rage or uncontrolled anger. If you're extremely angry, send your child to another room until you can calm down.

Parents should consider the true status of their child's heart when disciplining. How prideful are they? How rebellious? What will bring about true regret, repentance, and the best long-term result? What will help them quickly honor God's authority in the future? What will best curb their rebellion in later years? What will build their inner character? All children need lots of explanation and extended grace. When they misbehave out of ignorance, we should give them more mercy and teaching. But when a child understands and knows better, yet continues to act foolishly or rebelliously, the consequences of their actions should be greater and more stern (Luke 12:47–48).

If you see a child is quickly owning up to his or her mistakes, humbly showing remorse, and unlikely to repeat these same actions, your most effective path may be wisely demonstrating extra grace and less punishment. But if their track record is one of consistent misbehavior, and if past discipline has been too mild and ineffective, parents should be honest about what they may be reinforcing. The Bible says, "Discipline your son while there is hope" (Proverbs 19:18).

If children believe they can talk their way out of consequences or punishment by crying, negotiating, or manipulating, they will foolishly assume they can do so as an adult. By not firmly confronting rebellion early on, parents unwittingly lead them to many years of frustration and heartache. But if children are chastised lovingly and consistently when they are small, they will often rarely need it after the age of five or six.

> The rod and reproof give wisdom, but a child who gets his own way brings shame to his mother. . . . Correct your son, and he will give you comfort; he will also delight your soul. (Proverbs 29:15, 17)

APPENDIX II
12 daring ideas to maximize family time

1. *Declare war on the television*. The average American watches five hours of media a day. That's equivalent to nonstop viewing twenty-four hours a day for two months straight, every year—time that is usually wasted and non-interactive. Consider duct-taping the power button on your remote. This one decision can transform families.

2. *Play hooky*. Spontaneously show up and steal your kids away for lunch. Or talk ahead of time to their teachers so you can check them out early from school once or twice a year, even if just for a few hours in the afternoon. A day fishing with dad or shopping with mom while everyone is still in school is unbelievable to kids. Don't you wish your parents had done that for you?

3. *Pack up and leave town*. Families that camp together, even once a year, tend to closely bond. It forces you to work together to solve problems and then makes for hilarious stories you can laugh about later on. Buy a tent and find a state park. Learning how is half the fun.

4. *Establish radical interactive habits*. Read Deuteronomy 6:7 and observe the four activities that are in everyone's routine. Capture these conversation opportunities each day for your kids. Morning hugs, breakfast laughs, car catch-me-ups, bedtime tales, and tuck-me-in prayers—they all add up to years full of unregrettable moments.

5. *Start your own school*. Every year, more parents discover that homeschooling can be an exciting, effective alternative to government schools. By putting a child's training back into the hands of those who love them the most, homeschooling often

lowers a child's stress level, reinforces a family's faith and core values, opens up a family's traveling schedule, and prepares kids to handle greater responsibility in the future.

6. *Take your kids on business trips.* With a little bit of planning, you can get your kids' school assignments ahead of time and include them in your work travel. The fact that your business covers half the cost for you to take your child to a new city makes it that much more fun.

7. *Date your children.* Food is a sure way to take fellowship to the next level. So take your kids out on breakfast or dinner dates. Also, establish a family priority of making sure everyone stops what they're doing at night and eats meals together. Use this time to serve one another, ask questions, share stories, and get updates on how everyone is doing.

8. *Invite your sidekick to tag along.* Include your kids in what you are already doing. Let your housework or local errands include young helpers who can get candy at the register or ice cream on the way home. There's no need to leave them behind.

9. *Take Sundays off.* God commands families to take a day off for worship and rest each week. Let Sundays be a vacation day from your normal work and routine. Let church, an afternoon nap, and some focused family time recharge your home weekly on this special day.

10. *Launch family devotions.* Shutting down media for a few nights a week and getting everyone on the couch for a half-hour of rich conversation, prayer, and Scripture is an easy way to lead your family spiritually and invite God into your interaction. No preparation is needed. Just pray, read a chapter in the Bible, and enjoy discussing it together.

11. *Put your credit card in the freezer.* Parents who struggle with credit card debt often end up sacrificing time with their families so they can work the needed hours to make payments.

If you can't afford something without going into debt, ask yourself if it's really worth the cost. Make every effort to live on less. You're guarding your kids by waiting and paying with cash.

12. *Stop impressing your friends.* People often waste large amounts of time in their efforts to impress others. Kids don't need to play four instruments and six sports for you to brag on them. Choose one or two interest areas and spread things out so they don't become all-consuming. Winning awards at work is not worth failing at home. Be willing to let someone else get the plastic trophy this year so you can go home earlier at night.

APPENDIX III
How to pray for your children

We pray for you always, that our God will count you
worthy of your calling, and fulfill every desire for goodness
and the work of faith with power. (2 Thessalonians 1:11)

When you pray for your children, do you sometimes not know what to say? After you've asked God to bless them and take care of them, do you often just let it go at that?

Deep down we know that general prayers are actually lazy prayers—better than nothing perhaps, but not exactly the kind that show how much we love and care for our families.

The prayer themes on the following page capture more than a dozen specific requests that come straight from Scripture. We encourage you to look up the accompanying verses and to pray their promises over each of your kids, tailoring each item to what they're facing or handling at the time.

Sprinkle prayer for them throughout each month, rolling your prayers forward into a continuous stream of intercession that keeps your heart wanting nothing but God's best for each of them. As He gives you new things to pray about, add those to your list and keep track of how God responds and answers each one.

Not only does God promise to reward the person who prays persistently with believing faith (Matthew 7:7–8), but the habit of praying for each member of your family will help you keep them at the top of your priorities.

PRAY THAT THEY WILL:

1. Love the Lord their God with all their heart, soul, mind, and strength, and their neighbors as themselves. (Matt. 22:36–40)
2. Come to know Christ as Lord early in life. (2 Tim. 3:15)
3. Develop a hatred for evil, pride, hypocrisy, and sin. (Ps. 97:10; 38:18; Prov. 8:13)
4. Be protected from evil in each area of their lives: spiritually, emotionally, mentally, and physically. (John 17:15; 10:10; Rom. 12:9)
5. Be caught when they are guilty and receive the chastening of the Lord. (Ps. 119:71; Heb. 12:5–6)
6. Receive wisdom, understanding, knowledge, and discretion from the Lord. (Dan. 1:17, 20; Prov. 1:4; James 1:5)
7. Respect and submit to those in authority. (Rom. 13:1; Eph. 6:1–3; Heb. 13:17)
8. Be surrounded by the right kinds of friends and avoid wrong friends. (Prov. 1:10–16; 13:20)
9. Find a godly mate and raise godly children who will live for Christ. (2 Cor. 6:14–17; Deut. 6)
10. Walk in sexual and moral purity throughout their lives. (1 Cor. 6:18–20)
11. Keep a clear conscience that remains tender before the Lord. (Acts 24:16; 1 Tim. 1:19; 4:1–2; Titus 1:15–16)
12. Not fear any evil but walk in the fear of the Lord. (Ps. 23:4; Deut. 10:12)
13. Be a blessing to your family, the church, and the cause of Christ in the world. (Matt. 28:18–20; Eph. 1:3; 4:29)
14. Be filled with the knowledge of God's will and fruitful in every good work. (Eph. 1:16–19; Phil. 1:11; Col. 1:9)
15. Overflow with love, discern what is best, and be blameless until the day of Christ. (Phil. 1:9–10)

The locks and keys of prayer

Devote yourselves to prayer; stay alert in it with thanksgiving.
(Colossians 4:2)

THE LOCKS: TEN THINGS THAT BLOCK PRAYER

1. Praying without knowing God through Jesus.

John 14:6—Jesus said to him, "I am the way, and the truth, and the life; no one comes to the Father but through Me."

2. Praying from an unrepentant heart.

Psalm 66:18–19 NIV—"If I had cherished sin in my heart, the Lord would not have listened; but God has surely listened and heard my voice in prayer."

3. Praying for show.

Matthew 6:5—"When you pray, you are not to be like the hypocrites; for they love to stand and pray in the synagogues and on the street corners so that they may be seen by men. Truly I say to you, they have their reward in full."

4. Praying repetitive, empty words.

Matthew 6:7–8—"And when you are praying, do not use meaningless repetition as the Gentiles do, for they suppose that they will be heard for their many words. So do not be like them; for your Father knows what you need before you ask Him."

5. Prayers not prayed.

James 4:2—"You do not have because you do not ask."

6. Praying with a lustful heart.

James 4:3—"You ask and do not receive, because you ask with wrong motives, so that you may spend it on your pleasures."

7. Praying while mistreating your spouse.

1 Peter 3:7—"You husbands in the same way, live with your wives in an understanding way . . . and show her honor as a fellow heir of the grace of life, so that your prayers will not be hindered."

8. Praying while ignoring the poor.

Proverbs 21:13—"He who shuts his ear to the cry of the poor will also cry himself and not be answered."

9. Praying with bitterness in your heart toward someone.

Mark 11:25–26—"Whenever you stand praying, forgive, if you have anything against anyone, so that your Father who is in heaven will also forgive you your transgressions. But if you do not forgive, neither will your Father who is in heaven forgive your transgressions."

10. Praying with a faithless heart.

James 1:6–8—"But he must ask in faith without any doubting, for the one who doubts is like the surf of the sea, driven and tossed by the wind. For that man ought not to expect that he will receive anything from the Lord, being a double-minded man, unstable in all his ways."

THE KEYS: TEN THINGS THAT MAKE PRAYER EFFECTIVE

1. Praying by consistently asking, seeking, and knocking.

Matthew 7:7–8, 11—"Ask, and it will be given to you; seek, and you will find; knock, and it will be opened to you. For everyone who asks receives, and he who seeks finds, and to him who knocks it will be opened. . . . If you then, being evil, know how to give good gifts to your children, how much more will your Father who is in heaven give what is good to those who ask Him!"

2. Praying in faith.

Mark 11:24—"Therefore I say to you, all things for which you pray and ask, believe that you have received them, and they will be granted you."

3. Praying in secret.

Matthew 6:6—"But you, when you pray, go into your inner room, close your door and pray to your Father who is in secret, and your Father who sees what is done in secret will reward you."

4. Praying according to God's will.

1 John 5:14—"This is the confidence we have before Him, that, if we ask anything according to His will, He hears us."

5. Praying in Jesus' name.

John 14:13–14—"Whatever you ask in My name, that will I do, that the Father may be glorified in the Son. If you ask Me anything in My name, I will do it."

6. **Praying in agreement with other believers.**

Matthew 18:19–20—"Again I say to you, that if two of you agree on earth about anything that they may ask, it shall be done for them by My Father who is in heaven. For where two or three have gathered together in My name, I am there in their midst."

7. **Praying while fasting.**

Acts 14:23—"When they had appointed elders for them in every church, having prayed with fasting, they commended them to the Lord in whom they had believed."

8. **Praying from an obedient life.**

1 John 3:21–22—"Beloved, if our heart does not condemn us, we have confidence before God; and whatever we ask we receive from Him, because we keep His commandments and do the things that are pleasing in His sight."

9. **Praying while abiding in Christ and His Word.**

John 15:7—"If you abide in Me, and My words abide in you, ask whatever you wish, and it will be done for you."

10. **Praying while delighting in the Lord.**

Psalm 37:4—"Delight yourself in the LORD; and He will give you the desires of your heart."

SUMMARY OF THE LOCKS AND KEYS OF PRAYER

1. **You must be in a right relationship with God.**
2. **You must be in a right relationship with other people.**
3. **Your heart must be right.**

APPENDIX V
How to find peace with God

For He Himself is our peace. (Ephesians 2:14)

God created us to please and honor Him. But because of our own pride and selfishness, every one of us has fallen short of our purpose and dishonored God at different times in our lives. Whether it is us as parents or our children, we have all sinned against Him, failing to bring Him the credit, honor, and glory He deserves from each of us (Romans 3:23).

So if any of us claims to be a good person, we need to be honest with ourselves: Have we ever ignored God and failed to keep Him first in our lives? Have we ever disobeyed and dishonored Him by lying, cheating, lusting, stealing, rebelling against authorities, or hating others? Not only do these sins cause consequences in this life; they disqualify us from being right before God and living with Him in heaven for eternity.

God is holy, so He must reject all that is sinful (Matthew 13:41–43). And because He is perfect, He cannot allow us to sin against Him and go unpunished, or else He would not be a just judge (Romans 2:5–8). The Bible says that our sins separate us from God (Isaiah 59:2) and that the "wages of sin is death" (Romans 6:23). This death is not only physical but also spiritual, resulting in separation from God forever.

What most people don't realize is that our occasional good deeds do not take away our sins or somehow cleanse us in God's eyes. If they could, then we could earn our way into heaven, bypass the justice of God, and negate the punishment we deserve. This is not only impossible, but it denies God's character, His promises, and the honor He deserves. The good news, however, is that God is not only just, but He is also loving and merciful. He has provided a better way for us to have forgiveness and come to know Him.

Out of His love and kindness for us, the Bible says He sent His only Son, Jesus Christ, to come to earth, live a sinless life, and then shed His blood and die in our place to pay the price for our sins. This provided a pure sacrifice and a just payment to God for all we have done wrong, and it allowed Jesus to receive the judgment and punishment we deserve. Jesus' death satisfied the justice of God while also providing a perfect demonstration of the mercy and love of God. Three days after Jesus' death, God raised Him back to life just as He promised (Acts 13:26–43) and proved that He is the Son of God (Romans 1:4).

> God demonstrates His own love for us, in that while we were yet sinners, Christ died for us. (Romans 5:8)

> For God so loved the world, that He gave His only begotten Son, that whoever believes in Him should not perish, but have eternal life. (John 3:16)

Because of the death and resurrection of Jesus Christ, both we and our children are given the opportunity of being forgiven and finding peace with God. It may not seem right that salvation is a free gift. But the Scriptures teach that God wanted to reveal how rich His grace and kindness are toward us by offering us salvation for free (Ephesians 2:1–7). He is now commanding all people everywhere to repent (Acts 17:30–31), turn away from their sinful ways, and humbly trust Jesus for their salvation.

By surrendering your life to His lordship and control, you can have forgiveness and freely receive everlasting life.

The wages of sin is death, but the free gift of God is eternal life in Christ Jesus our Lord. (Romans 6:23)

Millions of people around the world have found peace with God through surrendering their lives to Jesus Christ. But each of us must choose for ourselves.

If you confess with your mouth Jesus as Lord, and believe in your heart that God raised Him from the dead, you will be saved. (Romans 10:9)

Is there anything stopping you from surrendering your life to Jesus right now? If you understand your need to be forgiven, and if you desire to begin a relationship with God, we encourage you to pray now, calling upon the name of Jesus and trusting your life to Him. Be honest with God about your mistakes and your need for His forgiveness. Resolve to turn away from your sin and to place your faith in Him and in what He did on the cross for you. Then open your heart and invite Him into your life to fill you, change your heart, and take control.

If you are not sure how to communicate this to Him, then use this prayer as a guide:

Lord Jesus, I know that I have sinned against You and deserve the judgment of God. I believe that You died on the cross to pay for my sins. I choose now to turn away from my sins and ask for Your forgiveness. Jesus, I am making You the Lord and Boss of my life. Fill my heart and take control. Change me and help me now to live the rest of my life for You. Thank You for giving me a home in heaven with You when I die. Amen.

If you just prayed sincerely and gave your life to Jesus Christ, then we congratulate you and encourage you to tell others about your decision. If you really meant it, then you need to take some important first steps in your new spiritual journey.

First, it is essential that you find a Bible-teaching church and tell them you want to obey Christ's command to make your faith public and be baptized. This is a great mile marker that allows you to openly identify with Jesus, share your faith with others, and launch your new spiritual walk. Plug into your new church and start attending on a regular basis, sharing life with other believers in Jesus Christ. They will encourage you, pray for you, and help you to grow. We all need encouragement, fellowship with one another, and accountability.

Also, find a Bible you can understand and begin to read it for a few minutes every day. Start in the book of John and work your way through the New Testament. As you read, ask God to teach you how to love Him and walk with Him. Begin to talk with God in prayer to thank Him for your new life, confess your sins when you fail, and ask Him for what you need.

As you walk with the Lord, take advantage of opportunities God gives you to share your faith with others. The Bible says, "In your hearts revere Christ as Lord. Always be prepared to give an answer to everyone who asks you to give the reason for the hope that you have" (1 Peter 3:15 NIV). There is no greater joy than to know God and to make Him known!

And as parents, it is an amazing privilege to be able to make Him known to our own children. If you have received God's forgiveness for your sins through faith and by His grace—whether now or many years ago—share this wonderful news with your family and children. If they haven't already done so, and if your children are old enough to understand, encourage them and invite them to join you on this journey of peace, joy, and lifelong purpose in Christ.

God has truly made a way for us to experience assurance and peace in Him. Of all the things we do not know or cannot predict about life, we can know for certain that He is with us now and that our souls are safe with Him forever.

God bless you as you live out and discover the truth of His promises, not only yourself but also with your entire family.

APPENDIX VI

Great verses for your children to memorize

Of all the things you want in your children's minds and hearts from now into adulthood, the words of Scripture offer the best guarantee of providing trusted guidance for every possible situation in life. Especially with your encouragement, these powerful truths from God's Word will stay with them, always available for the Holy Spirit to apply at just the right moment.

Scripture memory overwhelms some people. But like anything, if you put your mind to it, you can be more capable of memorizing than you realize. When people say they can't do it, they're really just saying they're not willing to work that hard. So set your goals high and make it a priority, and resolve to show your children how you will hide God's Word in your heart (Psalm 119:11).

Start enjoying the unity it can grow in your family as you commit verses to memory together. Let them become what you choose to think on as you drift off to sleep at night, drive to work, or run errands. They'll do a lot more good for you than oldies music and reruns. And you'll know you're giving your children a trusted inheritance of truth, knowledge, and lasting wisdom.

See the next page for a suggested list of outstanding verses, passages, and even whole chapters to memorize.

IMPORTANT TOPICS

Obeying parents (Ephesians 6:1–3)

Valuing God's Word (Psalm 119:11, 105)

Trusting God (Proverbs 3:5–6)

Surrendering to God (Romans 12:1; Luke 9:23)

Redeeming your time (Ephesians 5:15–16)

Doing justly and loving mercy (Micah 6:8)

Walking in wisdom (Ecclesiastes 12:1, 13–14)

Avoiding wrong friends (1 Corinthians 15:33)

Fighting temptation (1 Corinthians 10:13)

Empowered by Christ (Galatians 2:20; Philippians 4:13)

Confessing sin (Proverbs 28:13; 1 John 1:9)

Forgiving others (Ephesians 4:32)

Avoiding worry (Philippians 4:6–7)

Thinking pure thoughts (Philippians 4:6–8)

Knowing Jesus (John 3:16; 10:10; 14:6; 15:5)

LONGER PASSAGES

The Ten Commandments (Exodus 20:1–17)

The Romans Road (Romans 3:23; 5:8; 6:23; 10:9–10)

The Greatest Commandments (Matthew 22:36–40)

The Great Commission (Matthew 28:18–20)

The Model Prayer (Matthew 6:9–15)

The Armor of God (Ephesians 6:10–18)

The Nature of Love (1 Corinthians 13:4–8)

The Fruit of the Spirit (Galatians 5:22–23)

WHOLE CHAPTERS

Psalms 1; 15; 23; 91; 139

Proverbs 3

Romans 6; 8; 12

Ephesians 4; Philippians 4; Colossians 1; 2 Timothy 2

APPENDIX VII
Questions to ask your child

During a parent-child date or private conversation at home, use the questions below to learn more about the heart and life of your child. Allow this discussion to spark additional questions you may wish to explore, but keep the conversation very positive, emotionally safe, and open. Listen much more than you talk. "A plan in the heart of a man is like deep water, but a man of understanding draws it out" (Proverbs 20:5).

GENERAL

• How are you doing? What have you been up to lately?
• What are you really looking forward to in the next few weeks?
• What do you like the most about your life right now?
• What do you like the least about your life right now?
• Is there anything you are really stressed or worried about?

HOPES AND DREAMS

• What are some things you've always wanted to do one day?
• What do you wish your life could look like five years from now?
• If you could do anything at all and get paid for it, what would your dream job be?
• If you could spend a day with anyone in the world, who would it be and why?
• What is something you would really love to be given as a gift?
• If you had a million dollars, what would you do with it?

(continued on next page)

Love

- What have I done for you in the past that made you feel really loved?
- What could I do for you in the future that would help you feel loved?
- Of the following things, which would you enjoy the most?

  1. Being held or having your back rubbed for a while
  2. Sitting and talking for an hour about anything you would want to talk about
  3. Having someone serve you and help you work on a project you really want to do
  4. Hearing someone encourage you and share with you things they like about you
  5. Being given a nice gift

Parenting

- What are three things I do as a parent that you really like?
- What do you think would make me a better parent if I could change some things about myself?
- What are some things you would do differently when you parent your child one day?
- What words would you like to hear from me more often?
- Have I hurt you or wronged you in any way? Are you angry with me right now?
- Do you have any questions for me? Is there anything bothering you right now?
- How can I pray for you?

Heart to Heart

- Are you happy with your life right now?
- Do you like being in our family? Do you like being you?
- What have you been thinking about a lot lately?
- Who do you feel the most safe talking to and being around? Why?
- Has anyone ever hurt you, and you have not been able to forgive them?
- If you could go back in time, what are some things you would do differently?
- Is there anything you are afraid to tell me because of how you think I might respond?
- How are you doing in your relationship with God right now?
- What is the next decision that you think God would want you to make for Him?

Offer encouragement and a listening ear. Refuse to allow this to become an argument or opportunity for you to criticize. Let this be a time for your child to express themselves.

Know well the condition of your flock, and pay attention to your herds.
(Proverbs 27:23 HCSB)

The Word of God in my life

Let this proclamation help you to rightly approach the Word of God.

The Bible is the Word of God.

It is holy, inerrant, infallible, and completely authoritative. (*Proverbs 30:5–6; John 17:17; Psalm 119:89*)

It is profitable for teaching, reproving, correcting, and training me in righteousness. (*2 Timothy 3:16*)

It matures and equips me to be ready for every good work. (*2 Timothy 3:17*)

It is a lamp to my feet and a light to my path. (*Psalm 119:105*)

It makes me wiser than my enemies. (*Psalm 119:97–100*)

It brings me stability during the storms of my life. (*Matthew 7:24–27*)

If I believe its truth, I will be set free. (*John 8:32*)

If I hide it in my heart, I will be protected in times of temptation. (*Psalm 119:11*)

If I continue in it, I will become a true disciple. (*John 8:31*)

If I meditate on it, I will become successful. (*Joshua 1:8*)

If I keep it, I will be rewarded and my love perfected. (*Psalm 19:7–11; 1 John 2:5*)

It is the living, powerful, discerning Word of God. (*Hebrews 4:12*)

It is the sword of the Spirit. (*Ephesians 6:17*)

It is sweeter than honey and more desirable than gold. (*Psalm 19:10*)

It is indestructible and forever settled in Heaven. (*2 Corinthians 13:7–8; Psalm 119:89*)

It is absolutely true with no mixture of error. (*John 17:17; Titus 1:2*)

It is absolutely true about God. (*Romans 3:4; 16:25, 27; Colossians 1*)

It is absolutely true about man. (*Jeremiah 17:9; Psalm 8:4–6*)

It is absolutely true about sin. (*Romans 3:23*)

It is absolutely true about salvation. (*Acts 4:12; Romans 10:9*)

It is absolutely true about Heaven and Hell. (*Revelation 21:8; Psalm 119:89*)

Lord, open my eyes that I may see truth and my ears to hear truth.

Open my heart to receive it by faith.

Renew my mind to keep it in hope.

Surrender my will that I may live it with love.

Remind me that I am responsible when I hear it.

Help me desire to obey what You say through it.

Transform my life that I may know it.

Burden my heart that I may share it.

Speak now, Lord.

Give me a passion to know and follow Your will.

Nothing more. Nothing less. Nothing else.

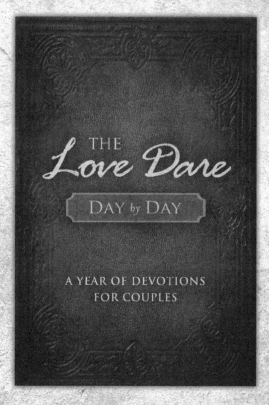

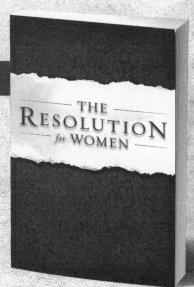

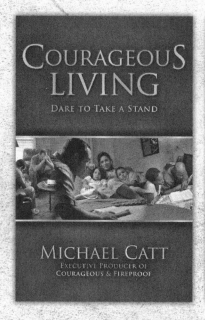